Here's What People Are Saying about this Resource:

"Bulls-eye! Marilyn Ross has scored a bulls-eye with her *National Directory of Newspaper Op-Ed Pages*. I consider it mandatory weaponry in the arsenal of any PR-minded guerilla."

–Jay Conrad Levinson, author
Guerilla Marketing

"It's a great tool for any writer who wants to shape public opinion."

–Judith Appelbaum, author
How to Get Happily Published

"Ross has tapped an area overlooked by most writer directories."

–Hiley Ward
Editor & Publisher

"A great way to get your products and services showcased and receive payment besides."

–Barbara Brabec, editor/publisher
Barbara Brabec's Self-Employment Survival Letter

"Marilyn Ross has produced another valuable resource for speakers, authors and entrepreneurs."

–*The Accidental Entrepreneur*

"Promo Prop For PR Practitioners."

–*Association Trends*

"Steady guidance on how to write your essay and optimum ways to present it to a newspaper. The 200-plus entries in the main section are the result of a poll of op-ed editors."

–Bruce Rosenstein
"USA Today" Library*Library Journal*

"Identifies receptive newspapers in every U.S. state and all Canadian provinces, and gives full editorial contact information."

–*IABC Communication World*

"Even if you don't write op-ed pieces, it (*National Directory of Newspaper Op-Ed Pages*) gives you addresses and phone numbers of more than 200 newspapers for self-syndicating other features and columns."

–*Freelance Writer's Report*

"This guide shows you how to break into newsprint—without having to become a reporter or even write like one—through the lucrative opportunities of the op-ed page."

–*Writer's Digest Book Club Bulletin*

NATIONAL DIRECTORY OF NEWSPAPER OP-ED PAGES

by Marilyn Ross

A new, profitable tool for:
- **FREELANCE WRITERS**
- **PUBLIC RELATIONS PRACTITIONERS**
- **ASSOCIATIONS & NONPROFIT ORGANIZATIONS**
- **CORPORATE COMMUNICATIONS DEPARTMENTS**
- **SPEAKERS, AUTHORS, PROFESSORS, ENTREPRENEURS**

COMMUNICATION CREATIVITY
P.O. Box 909
Buena Vista, CO 81211

First printing 1994.
Second printing 1994.

Library of Congress Cataloging-in-Publication Date

Ross, Marilyn Heimberg.
   National directory of newspaper Op-Ed pages / by Marilyn Ross.
     p. cm.
   The National survey of newspaper Op-Ed pages was updated and renamed the National directory of newspaper Op-Ed pages in 1994.
   Includes index.
   ISBN 0-918880-17-3 : $19.95
   1. American newspapers--Sections, columns, etc.--Op-Ed pages--Directories. 2. Journalism--Authorship--Marketing--Directories.
I. National survey of newspaper "Op-Ed" pages. II. Title.
PN4888.073R66 1994
070.4'42-dc20   94-17060
          CIP

Design, typesetting, and printing services provided by About Books, Inc., 425 Cedar Street, Buena Vista, CO 81211, 800-548-1876.

ATTENTION COLLEGES & UNIVERSITIES, PROFESSIONAL ORGANIZATIONS AND CORPORATIONS: Quantity discounts are available on bulk purchases of this directory for educational purposes or fund raising. Special books or book excerpts can also be created to fit specific needs. For information, please contact Special Sales Department, Communication Creativity, P.O. Box 909, Buena Vista, CO 81211-0909, or call 719-395-8659.

TABLE OF CONTENTS

INTRODUCTION

This directory evolved out of a need. One of our consulting clients wanted to gain national exposure and enhance her reputation. While she was already an expert in her field, our goal was to get her even more visibility and credibility. One of the ideas we hit upon was writing Op-Ed pieces.

The "Op-Ed" (short for opposite editorial) page refers to a physical location rather than an analytical position. It doesn't mean that articles oppose the editorial point of view of the paper, rather it literally denotes where these pieces are found: opposite the editorial page.

This is a forum for opinion and observation that has come into its own over the last couple of decades. It's a place where grass-roots go-getters mingle with political pundits, where many people have their "public say." It's not just a place to rebut, settle accounts, serve notice, or exact revenge. Op-Ed page editors need fresh voices with new thoughts, classy writing, mind-bending revelation. "I like to think of the Op-Ed page as the people's page," says Diane Clark of *The San Diego Union Tribune.* It's where an informed outsider is granted a forum.

"We consider our Commentary page as a marketplace of ideas," reports Phil Joyce who is with the *Philadelphia Inquirer.* The Op-Ed page is a vehicle for an intellectual transaction between writer and reader, believes Richard Liefer of the *Chicago Tribune.* He calls it "A meeting place of the minds." Many feel the page is at it's best when it gives a voice to people who don't usually have one, or who don't usually choose it use it.

Back in 1986, when I embarked on a search to learn where there was a national directory or compendium of information on the subject, it turned into quite a journey. A call to *Editor & Publisher* magazine revealed they had no such information, but perhaps the American Newspaper Publishers Association would. While they were very gracious, they didn't have the data either. After being referred to the Society of Newspaper Editors, the National Conference of Editorial Writers, and the American Society of Newspaper Editors, I was about to give up. Then a gentleman at the Newspaper Advertising Bureau came to the rescue. He had an old 1983 list of the names of all the papers in the country that carried Op-Ed material. The names. Period.

So my work began in earnest. I culled from this list some 170 papers with circulations of at least 40,000 and looked up all the addresses. Next I fired off 170 letters with specific questions inquiring about their current needs. Soon self-addressed, stamped envelopes were choking our mail box. It was only when I had dozens and dozens of responses, many of them with helpful personal notes from editors, that I realized this was valuable one-of-a-kind information that should be shared.

Thus the *National Survey of Newspaper Op-Ed Page Editors* was born. Purchasers of that first limited survey have begged for an update. So we began the process again, only on a much wider scale, in 1994. Additional information-gathering mailings, endless phone calls, and extensive research resulted in a one-of-a-kind reference that is cogent, current, and comprehensive.

Renamed the *National Directory of Newspaper Op-Ed Pages*, it serves a multitude of functions for several groups of people. It's designed to aid media planners seeking a particular kind of editorial environment for their message, as well as freelancers looking for new paying markets, and authors wanting to tout the subject of their newest books. It also meets the needs of think tanks and colleges and universities who seek a forum.

Actually the title of *National Directory of Newspaper Op-Ed Pages* is a misnomer. Purchasers of this directory get a bonus as it actually covers all of North America. Those living in the Canadian provinces, or wanting to submit there, will find information about key Canadian newspapers included as well. I've also included a section that discusses fertile fields for essays in consumer magazines and trade journals.

Freelance writers discover in this directory new markets all across North America. Of equal appeal, because of the immediacy of newspapers, these writers no longer have to submit a query or an article—then wait months to learn if an editor is interested. Newspapers make decisions in days not months. And in many cases you can self-syndicate your material, offering exclusive rights in several circulation areas simultaneously. Op-Ed pieces can make the difference between bare survival and financial comfort.

Some papers pay at the rate of about 30 cents per word, some not at all, a few as much as $250 per piece. If you're a neophyte looking to amass clips, consider the non-paying markets that help you get samples of your work into print.

PR and advertising professionals discover within these pages fresh opportunities to promote industries, ideas, and individuals. By taking advantage of Op-Ed page exposure, a creative professional can develop a concerted campaign to rally public attention or mold public opinion for his or her client. Often a business concept can piggyback on a news event or anniversary, giving it timeliness and relevancy.

One Los Angeles PR executive I spoke with commented he thought this was an "overlooked area." He felt it could add significantly to credibility. A leading Philadelphia firm had this to say, "As public relations professionals we believe that the opinion pages of daily newspapers and other publications allows our clients to take an active roll in the media, much more so than simply being 'written about.'"

Book authors will find here a venue ideal for addressing their passions. And since most Op-Ed pieces carry a bio line, your book can be plugged as you sound off about topics close to your heart. With newspaper review space at a premium, and competition for off-the-book pages extremely competitive, a citation in the editorial pages can yield dramatic results, as we explain later.

Professional speakers and CEOs who give keynotes are often on the cutting edge of important issues. Repackaging your acumen can pay big dividends. Winnow the crux of your speech to a powerful 700-800 words—and gain new credibility and visibility.

Corporate communication departments and entrepreneurs seeking higher profiles and profits will find that by sharing their professional views on the Op-Ed pages, they gain more respect and are perceived as having more clout. Reprints of pieces authored by business leaders make impressive additions to proposals aimed at investors, bankers, customers, or clients. And they are powerful additions to annual reports and media kits.

Associations, nonprofit organizations, think tanks, and government officials will find the Op-Ed pages ideal showcases to lobby for their causes. As recognized experts in their fields, executive directors and spokespersons can offer pertinent and insightful commentary on events, issues, surveys, or trends touching on their areas. One think tank plans to use broadcast fax technology to send Op-Ed pieces to several hundred regional weekly and bi-weekly newspapers. These weeklies have enormous reach and penetration and are perceived as an important way to communicate with a wide audience.

College and university professors who suffer from the need to "publish or perish" will discover within these pages guidance for getting their names into print in places beyond academic journals. Campus experts can find full details about appropriate outlets in newspapers and magazines for discussions about their interesting work and unusual stories. Educators are a rich source for thought-provoking material about their specialties.

PART I

WHAT IT'S ALL ABOUT

THE HOWS AND WHYS OF OP-ED PAGES

Op-Ed pages are a public bulletin board for poignant critiques. And they are growing in importance. Op-Ed editors say their pages are increasingly managed independently of the traditional editorial page editor and have grown in size and reader popularity. In a move that symbolized their burgeoning significance, these editors from around the country met in Minnesota in 1990 to take a serious look at launching an association. Shortly thereafter the National Association of Op-Ed Page Editors was born.

Certainly Herbert Bayard Swope, who is credited with actually inventing Op-Ed pages in a now defunct New York newspaper in 1921, couldn't have dreamed they would flourish so. The modern version of the Op-Ed page was started about 25 years ago by *The New York Times*. On September 21, 1970, Op-Ed pages got a further boost. That day *The Times* announced it would devote additional space to serve as a forum for exploring issues and new ideas by writers and thinkers from outside *The Times*. "Diverse voices of society must be given the greatest possible opportunity to be heard," they declared.

Particularly as more cities have only one newspaper, Op-Ed pages serve to ensure that a wider range of voices has an outlet that isn't tainted with the surviving paper's stand on issues. The *St. Louis Post Dispatch* didn't have an Op-Ed page until the demise of the *Globe Democrat* in 1984, for instance. Before that, generations of St. Louis residents had easy access to sharply contrasting views. When the conservative newspaper in the community was silenced, the remaining paper decided the time was right to give more formal space to opposing views. Other cities are following suit.

The April 23, 1994 issue of *Editor & Publisher* tells of a Spokane, Washington, newspaper that has appointed new "interactive" editors to scour the community for individuals to write for the opinion pages. The *Spokesman-Review* has taken a bold step listening actively to their readership about issues that matter in their lives. They have even formed focus groups seeking ideas. One of their first submissions was from a seventh-grader who told about deaths in her family that had resulted from drugs. She touted the DARE program and how it keeps kids off drugs and alcohol. Another time a man and woman wrote of their differing reactions as they watched parents abusing children in public.

Today's ever-growing pages, considered by many a must-read, offer an unprecedented opportunity. One of the wonderful aspects of

Op-Eds is that editors of these pages *actually read* the submissions they receive. Unlike most magazine editors and many of those responsible for other pages or sections of newspapers, Op-Ed editors not only genuinely crave good material, they are willing to personally sample what comes in.

I appreciate their generosity of spirit in so graciously completing our surveys and talking with us on the phone. Otherwise we couldn't have created a directory that puts them together with the individuals who supply their products: freelance writers, PR people, corporate communications directors, book authors, speakers, CEOs, college and university professors, and others with something important to say.

Op-Ed pages are a spectacular sounding board for legislative issues or to conduct public policy debates. They are a powerful way to lobby Congress. For many they represent free advertising. For others they afford an opportunity to inform, persuade, satirize. They typically offer a biting, funny, or touching dialogue with non-traditional voices.

Pay for these pieces ranges from nothing to a thousand dollars. It sometimes varies at the same paper. Hot topics may command more than run-of-the mill stuff. (In one case, it depends *where on the page* your piece appears.) Several editors reward you more generously after you make your first sale to them.

Length is as varied as spring wild flowers. Some will take as few as 400 words, others allow you 1200. One magazine wants pieces from 4,000 to 6,000 words. For most newspapers, 700 words is the norm.

Timeliness often dictates what essays will appear. Monitor what's going on in the news carefully and seize the moment. Respond immediately if you have an idea that ties in with a current event. A week later the subject will probably be dead. Faxing or calling is wise when you're suggesting an especially timely piece. Make the immediacy of the piece obvious in the title or lead paragraph.

Sid Hurlburt, who presides over the Guest Columns for *USA Today*, wants pieces that express an opinion and perspective on the previous day's news. If he goes for your idea and makes the assignment, you must be prepared to deliver a polished piece in about six *hours*. He recommends that PR practitioners send a brief memo containing background information on the client, the issue, and the client's position.

Extraordinary things can result from an Op-Ed. A few years ago the Op-Ed page of *The New York Times* printed a piece extolling the desirable simplicity of earlier times and how modern inventions are not so terrific after all. A literary agent who read the essay was struck by the literary skill with which it was written. He was determined to locate the author. The result was a contract with Harper for a book of previously published and new essays—which was published on Mother's Day when the author was a mere 96 years old.

A *Newsweek* "My Turn" essay attacking the college loan pay-back system not only helped its author pay off those loans, it helped him get a job at the *Washington Monthly* and led to his becoming a contributing editor to the magazine.

The leading bulk trucking company in the U.S.—which logs over three million miles a year on the nation's highways as the major carrier for the chemical, food, petroleum, forest products, and building industries—used Op-Ed pages to rally support for one of its concerns. At the time a bill was before Congress that would allow individual states to raise the nationwide 55 mile-an-hour speed limit to 70 mph on interstate highways outside major urban areas.

A safety conscious company, the trucking firm believed raising the speed limit was wrong. The president wrote an editorial that appeared in over 100 daily newspapers and trade magazines and reached an audience of well over 8 million readers . . . many of whom were legislators destined to vote on that bill.

In another case, a manufacturer of industrial vacuums for toxic, hazardous, and nuisance waste used Op-Ed pages to defend the cause of one of it's customers. It conducts a major portion of its business in asbestos abatement equipment. Asbestos abatement contractors had lost, or been unable to obtain, liability insurance because of the nature of their work.

The president of the vacuum manufacturer spoke out on the issue of asbestos liability insurance and the need for a solution to the problem. His piece received excellent reception from daily newspapers across the country, plus various trade magazines ran it. The editorial was instrumental in making the general public aware that asbestos removal must continue and qualified contractors must be insured in order to remove this potentially hazardous material.

The list of success stories goes on and on.

CRAFTING COMPELLING ESSAYS

Syndicated columnist James J. Kilpatrick observed that perhaps half of all columns "are pontifical, portentous, pointless; their writers boil not, neither do they grin. They merely plod."

Be a flame thrower rather than one who timidly lights a pilot. Earn the right to see your byline on the Op-Ed page by the strength of your argument, the appeal of your subject, and the quality of your writing.

Forget the middle road. It's booooooorrring. Your challenge is to make people view things from a different angle. The best compliment an Op-Ed page editor can receive is "you made me think." They want a good mix: a balance between the weighty and the whimsical, the expected and the surprising. They're seeking more than warmed-over work from news services. They need views to satisfy a broad range of reader tastes. This is a place where controversy can bloom, where blandness is forbidden, and reader's blood pressure rises.

Because the competition goes up as the circulation numbers increase, however, it behooves contributors to write the most forceful piece possible. Said an editor at *Newsday*, "We look for clarity of language and logic as well as freshness of approach." Find a creative slant. Offer facts the paper hasn't used before. Take a strong position.

Use vibrant language. Consider analogy or metaphor to give your piece an offbeat flavor. If applicable, insert a couple of potent statistics to add validity to your case.

One of the best ways to score is by developing a local hook to a major national event or anniversary date. A broad-brush approach will only work with the national dailies. Otherwise, if you tie in a local person, institution, or event to a topic of general relevance, you'll hit a home run more often. Many papers are reluctant to accept submissions from people living outside of their immediate area. In this situation it's vital you find a local angle if you want serious consideration.

For inspiration scan a directory called *Chase's Annual Events.* It lists more than 10,000 entries that cover holidays and holy days, special events, historic birth and death dates, ethnic celebrations, festivals, battles, presidential proclamations, you name it. This publication is a gold mine of facts, fresh ideas, and special reasons you can piggyback on.

A hospital manager of public relations found a good hook for a piece he ghostwrote for the chairman of psychiatry. Titled "5 Myths About Mental Illness Block Public Understanding," he tied it in with the approach of the new year and that traditionally this is a time to commit to self-improvement. He further postulated it was fitting, as we make plans for our own improvement, that we consider helping ourselves and others learn more about mental illness. Then he proceeded to shoot holes in popularly held assumptions.

When choosing a subject, write about your passion. If you feel strongly about something, chances are you'll write a convincing essay about it. Be sure you present your credentials in a strong cover letter. Most Op-Ed pieces are the purview of guest experts on important issues of the day. If you've got the background to write about a topic, flaunt it!

Also look to the commonplace as well as the profound. Some provocative pieces examine an aspect of our everyday lives without the weight of public policy being figured in. They take a more person-in-the-street approach. Specialists in nothing more than clear thinking have a good chance here. Sometimes short meditations on the mundane are a welcome relief from substantive discourses on the ills of the world.

If you want to leap from the slush pile, present an interesting case. Send in opposing views. Appropriate Op-Ed topics are as varied as Campbell soups: science, consumer concerns, education, social trends, minority and women's issues, technology, humor, and topics of local appeal. Also study the daily versus the Sunday Op-Ed pages. Some newspapers provide for longer analytic pieces on Sundays or offer a forum for greater diversity of subjects on the weekend.

Phil Joyce, Commentary page editor for the *Philadelphia Inquirer* and founding president of the National Association of Op-Ed Page Editors, offers this observation: "If we get two Op-Ed pieces and one agrees with our editorial position and the other one is opposed to it, we probably will pick the one in opposition." His reasoning is that there should be room for other viewpoints.

Be proactive rather than reactive. A forward-thinking freelancer or PR practitioner anticipates. For instance, is Congress voting on a bill of importance to you or one of your clients? Then have a "reaction" piece already in the hands of a key Op-Ed editor *before* the vote.

Joyce also encourages writers to look within their regional or local area for story ideas, such as education programs that are helping other schools or medical care problems that are being creatively solved.

One freelancer who has fine success with this medium advises putting your argument right up front. It's got to grab interest immediately. And if you're writing a piece of national scope, be aware the guy in Denver—who's bouncing his baby son while downing his morning Cheerios—needs to be able to relate.

Be careful about self-aggrandizing. If you become blatant about mentioning the title of your book, company, or product, it will be edited out totally. Instead, sign the cover letter with your name and book title or company. Include it in a bio blurb as well, of course.

Target your essays carefully. Your chances for success will be greatly enhanced if you study your market. Determine a paper's demographics and political leanings. Read the Op-Ed pages of the papers you expect to sell to or the magazines you're aiming for. Determine their tone. Do they print light pieces, or is everything on serious topics? Are they sophisticated or down-home? While a medieval analogy might charm a well-read audience, a sports comparison could work better for less literate readers. Are national and international events covered by syndicated columnists? Most papers have well known writers addressing key national topics. Therefore, they won't want your views on these issues unless you're offering an insightful counterpoint.

Do they cover just local and regional topics, or are informative and thoughtful pieces on wider trends and issues also included? Perhaps their scope extends to a section of the country, such as New England or the Rocky Mountain region. If you've done your homework—matching your piece with the paper's tone—and you present an analytical and stimulating viewpoint, chances are excellent your work will frequently grace the Op-Ed pages of the nation's leading newspapers.

USING THIS DIRECTORY FOR MAXIMUM RESULTS

First, let us address the format used to present the information. Papers are listed alphabetically by state, then by city, then by paper name. The one exception to this: the national papers, which are cited first.

You'll find complete addresses, the name of the proper editor to contact, phone and fax numbers, payment rates, desired length, if the paper is copyrighted, whether they require contributors to live within their circulation area, and when the Op-Ed pages appear.

The individual editorial comments included make this directory especially useful. Many editors went out of their way to provide guidance and cite their specific needs. Equally valuable is the feedback received from many freelancers and PR professionals. Many of my ASJA colleagues and others responded to a national call for input. Their comments provide insights and networking tidbits seldom shared.

Now let's examine the actual submission process. Material should be typed, double-spaced, and on white 8½-inch x 11-inch paper. Include a brief cover letter stating what subject your piece addresses, your writing credits (if any) or other appropriate credentials that equip you to deal with the subject. Also include your social security number (or Federal ID number) and both a day and evening phone number. Editors sometimes need to contact the author of an article for editing or verification purposes and must have a fast way of reaching you.

If you are offering exclusive rights in a particular area, this should also be noted. And if the paper isn't copyrighted, be sure to put the copyright symbol or the word "copyright," the year, and your name on your manuscript. Your package should always include a self-addressed, stamped envelope (SASE) for the enclosure of a check or your returned manuscript. Some PR firms that woo space on the editorial pages both fax and mail their submissions. A few even have them delivered by messenger to attract more attention.

You'll notice some of the papers require contributors to live in their circulation area. One approach associations or organizations with a national base can use is to create a piece in-house, then ask members who live in different papers' circulation areas to give it a local tie and submit it under their names and addresses.

Follow up techniques differ from most submissions. With this medium, response is usually forthcoming promptly. Wait at least a week before you follow up. Then do so by faxing or mailing your submission again. Keep it brief. They don't have the time or inclination to read fancy press kits. It you still haven't heard after a reasonable time, try a phone call. A final bit of advice is that if you must call an Op-Ed page editor, refrain from doing so on Thursdays or Fridays. These two days are particularly hectic.

Be aware of territorial exclusivity requirements. Most big-city dailies require what is called territorial exclusivity. This means they will have exclusive use of your material within their circulation area. In the past, this practice was sometimes abused. *Editor & Publisher* reports the *Milwaukee Journal* used to request exclusivity on syndicated offerings for all 72 counties in Wisconsin! And the *Seattle Times* previously bought exclusive rights from the Canadian border to the north to the Oregon border to the south, plus a big east-west chunk of the state of Washington.

Things are better today. But be aware if you submit something to the *Detroit Free Press*, for instance, you can't also send it to the *Detroit News*. Of course, if it is of national interest, there's nothing stopping you from selling it to more papers in other areas as long as each knows it is buying only rights in their area. Any of the three national papers would be justifiably miffed, however, if they saw a piece identical to one they bought appearing elsewhere.

It's important you honor exclusivity. Today papers often fax statements for writers to sign about exclusivity in their area. They stipulate where they're buying rights for.

I suspect with the growth of electronic transmission, that electronic rights will appear on most of these agreements in the future. This is good news for PR types whose mission is to "spread the word," not so good for freelancers who depend on selling their writing for a living.

Craft your biography tag line carefully. Many papers carry a sentence or two about each author of their Op-Ed pieces. Give this as much thought as you did the whole piece! You can't say much, so each word must count. If the story relates to a book you've recently written, be sure to state the title and publisher. If it is about a product, service, or company, identify the item or firm—and where it's located. If you're a freelancer, say that, what you specialize in writing about, and where you live. That way if someone is especially impressed with your piece, they can track you down. Here's an example of a forceful bio:

> Entertainment public relations executive (name), author of (book and publisher), a reference book, lives in Los Angeles.

Think about your personal and professional agenda and use this valuable space to promote yourself or your business effectively.

Also consider magazines that accept essays. Once you've gotten the hang of writing newspaper Op-Ed pieces, you may want to expand your horizons to include consumer magazines and trade journals. The pay for certain consumer publications escalates dramatically.

Newsweek's "My Turn" is coveted by anyone hungering for national exposure and a fat check. They pay $1,000 for a one-page essay! Begun in 1972 by then editor Osborn Elliott, "My Turn" was created to open *Newsweek's* pages to ordinary citizens as well as leading public figures. More recent essay contributors run the gamut from postal clerks to battered women, alcoholics to cops. The one thing they all have in common is the ability to voice their opinions articulately. Some take a humorous approach, others are angry. All feel passionately about their subjects. The competition to get Olwen

Clarke's (212-350-4547) attention is tough—he receives about 500 submissions a month—but the reward can be worth the effort. *Newsweek's* circulation exceeds three million, topping both the *Wall Street Journal* and *USA Today* by huge margins.

At the opposite end of the spectrum, one writer told me, "I once hit a button with the editor of *Playgirl* magazine when I wrote about how the tourism industry should promote environmental protection in its own self-interest. He ran it and I chuckled over this venue all the way to the bank." Another viable market is *Harper's Magazine,* which publishes one major essay per issue. In this case you can spin a lengthy yarn as their requirements run from 4,000 to 6,000 words and they generally pay a generous 50 cents to $1.00 per word. They look for topical essays on subjects ranging from politics to crime, the arts to business. The author must "bring the force of passionately informed statement."

Another writer told of selling Op-Ed pieces to the *Daily Shipping Guide,* a publication that covers transportation and transportation infrastructure in the southeast. They also take Op-Eds on taxes and other business topics, pay $2.35 an inch, and get checks out every two weeks. "They've purchased several editorials from me as a regular correspondent," she reports.

The Writer takes essays for "Off the Cuff" and the editor is said to be wonderful to work with. They pay $75 to $100. The *American Journalism Review* (formerly the *Washington Journalism Review*) accepts essays and pays a minimum of 20 cents per word. *Atlantic Monthly* is another possibility for upscale writing; so is *National Geographic Traveler.* Of course, many of the women's magazines offer essay possibilities. If you're willing to settle for clips instead of coins, literary magazines are another outlet. And the "back pages" of various publications welcome humorous essays and sometimes nostalgia, thus offering a new outlet for creators of such material to exhibit their talents.

Whether it's magazines or newspapers, I hope you find this philosophy behind Op-Ed page submissions useful and that the *National Directory of Newspaper Op-Ed Pages* will lead to many opportunities to see your work in print. Don't give up easily. Editors can be a quaint bunch; what one hates another may love.

In the process, won't you share any "insider secrets" you glean for the benefit of future readers? Those who contribute insights I can use receive a complimentary copy of the next edition of this directory when it's updated. Let me hear from you. Good luck and happy writing!

Part II

U.S. Newspapers

NATIONAL PAPERS

CHRISTIAN SCIENCE MONITOR
Kristiana Helmick, Op-Ed Coordinator
One Norway Street
Boston, MA 02115-3195

PAY SCALE: $100 base rate, goes up for repeat contributors
WORD LENGTH: 500-900 words, occasionally longer
COPYRIGHTED: They need exclusive 90-day worldwide rights
MUST LIVE IN AREA: not applicable
FREQUENCY: Mon-Fri
PHONE NUMBER: 617-450-2372
FAX NUMBER: 617-450-2317

COMMENTS: Open to any subjects except medical, liquor, or tobacco. Include a two or three line biographical blurb.

NEWSDAY

Noel Rubinton, Op-Ed Page Editor
235 Pinelawn Road
Long Island, NY 11747-4250

PAY SCALE: $150-400
WORD LENGTH: 500-700
COPYRIGHTED: first and one-time rights
MUST LIVE IN AREA: not applicable
FREQUENCY: Mon-Sat
PHONE NUMBER: 516-843-2900
FAX NUMBER: 516-843-2986

COMMENTS: The paper tries to give an edge in payment to those who write for a living. Coverage is local to international. Any subject is possible. "We use a tremendous amount of material in any given week so if you don't read the paper you're at a disadvantage," says Rubinton. They are happy to receive submissions that are in opposition or provocative. Rubinton looks for the unexpected and topical. He also "prefers that you be in front of something rather than on top of it." *Newsday* has two papers; they are joined at the hip. They have similarities but much is at a different slant. This Long Island *Newsday* runs local, state, and national. (The New York city *Newsday* runs city-related material.) Note that the daily "Viewpoint" section pays differently than the Sunday "Currents." The Sunday column pays $300-400 and the length can also be longer: 1,000-1,500 words. Rubinton suggests that you send a piece or two and later discuss queries over the phone. It is okay to call with questions, but he prefers fax or mail. Your piece will be returned only if an SASE is enclosed. "If you haven't heard in two weeks forget it," says Rubinton.

PACIFIC NEWS SERVICE

Sandy Close
450 Mission Street, Room 506
San Francisco, CA 94105

PAY SCALE: $100 first time, $150 thereafter
WORD LENGTH: 650-1000 words
COPYRIGHTED: yes, they want exclusive rights
MUST LIVE IN AREA: not applicable
FREQUENCY: daily
PHONE NUMBER: 415-243-4364
FAX NUMBER: 415-243-0815

COMMENTS: This is a wire service that syndicates material to subscribers all over the U.S. and some foreign countries. They look for an individual perspective on topics the writer is passionate about.

USA TODAY
Sid Hurlburt, Editors/Columns
1000 Wilson Boulevard
Arlington, VA 22229

PAY SCALE: $125
WORD LENGTH: 400
COPYRIGHTED: yes
MUST LIVE IN AREA: not applicable
FREQUENCY: Mon-Fri
PHONE NUMBER: 703-276-3400
FAX NUMBER: 703-558-3935
VOICE MAIL: 1-800-828-0909

COMMENTS: Hurlburt welcomes "guest columns" for the Op-Ed page. He wants the page to reflect diversity in geography, ideologies, and demographics. Typically, pieces express an opinion and perspective on the previous day's news. He offers the following suggestions for PR practitioners wanting bylines for their clients: To pitch a column, send a brief memo containing background information on the client, the issue, and the client's position. Be prepared to respond in six hours if he gives the go-ahead.

THE WALL STREET JOURNAL
Melanie Kirkpatrick, Op-Ed Page Editor
World Financial Center
200 Liberty Street
New York, NY 10281

PAY SCALE: 3 figures
WORD LENGTH: 800-1,500
COPYRIGHTED: yes
MUST LIVE IN AREA: not applicable
FREQUENCY: Mon-Fri
PHONE NUMBER: 212-416-2556
FAX NUMBER: 212-416-2658

COMMENTS: Covers a wide range of subjects, also receptive to shorter "slice of life" essays.

STATE PAPERS

DISTRICT OF COLUMBIA

WASHINGTON POST
Meg Greenfield, Editorial Page Editor
1150 15th Street NW
Washington, DC 20071-0002

PAY SCALE: do pay, but won't discuss range
WORD LENGTH: 850-1,000
COPYRIGHTED: yes
MUST LIVE IN AREA: no
FREQUENCY: daily
PHONE NUMBER: 202-334-6000
FAX NUMBER: 202-334-4344

COMMENTS: They have a very busy department and the information above was compiled from an information line (202-334-4855). They request a day and evening phone number, a return address, and an SASE. They will return your piece in 3-5 days if they don't use it. You can check the status of your essay by calling 202-334-7471.

WASHINGTON TIMES

Mary Lou Forbes, Op-Ed Page Editor
3600 New York Avenue, NE
Washington, DC 20002-1996

PAY SCALE: $100-200
WORD LENGTH: 700-1,000
COPYRIGHTED: no
MUST LIVE IN AREA: no
FREQUENCY: Mon-Fri
PHONE NUMBER: 202-636-3000
FAX NUMBER: 202-269-3419

COMMENTS:

ALABAMA

BIRMINGHAM NEWS
Justin Fox, Op-Ed Page Editor
2200 North Fourth Avenue
Birmingham, AL 35202-3840

PAY SCALE: $50
WORD LENGTH: 600-800, 1,000 + for Sunday's paper
COPYRIGHTED: first time rights
MUST LIVE IN AREA: no
FREQUENCY: daily
PHONE NUMBER: 205-325-2222
FAX NUMBER: 205-325-2283

COMMENTS: Fox's attention gets captured both by and about Alabama, and southern pieces in particular. They sometimes pay but it is determined case by case. For longer Sunday column or uncommon pieces they will pay more.

BIRMINGHAM POST HERALD
Karl Seitz, Op-Ed Page Editor
2200 Fourth Avenue, N.
Birmingham, AL 35203

PAY SCALE: seldom
WORD LENGTH: no longer than 2½ pages double-spaced
COPYRIGHTED: yes, but by state law writer holds rights
MUST LIVE IN AREA: preferred
FREQUENCY: 5 days a week
PHONE NUMBER: 205-325-2342
FAX NUMBER: 205-325-2410

COMMENTS:

MOBILE PRESS
Ralph Poore, Editorial Page Editor
304 Government Street
Mobile, AL 36630-0002

PAY SCALE: upper limit for solicited piece is $150
WORD LENGTH: 800-1,500
COPYRIGHTED: yes
MUST LIVE IN AREA: no, if an expert—prefer local submissions
FREQUENCY: daily, Sunday Commentary Section
PHONE NUMBER: 205-433-1551
FAX NUMBER: 205-434-8662

COMMENTS: Poore accepts a wide range of subjects and looks for "whatever is topical."

ALASKA

ANCHORAGE DAILY NEWS
Michael Carey, Op-Ed Page Editor
P.O. Box 149001
Anchorage, AK 99514-9001

PAY SCALE: $50-100 (rarely pays $100)
WORD LENGTH: 600-700
COPYRIGHTED: first time rights
MUST LIVE IN AREA: no
FREQUENCY: daily
PHONE NUMBER: 907-257-4200
FAX NUMBER: 907-258-2157

COMMENTS: Carey prefers you live in the area, but if you have special expertise and write on a topic pertinent to Alaska, you have a chance for submission.

ARIZONA

ARIZONA REPUBLIC
Stephanie Robertson, Perspective Editor
120 East Van Buren Street
Phoenix, AZ 85004-2227

PAY SCALE: seldom
WORD LENGTH: 700
COPYRIGHTED: yes
MUST LIVE IN AREA: yes
FREQUENCY: daily
PHONE NUMBER: 602-271-8292
FAX NUMBER: 602-271-8933

COMMENTS:

PHOENIX GAZETTE
James Hill, Editorial Page Editor
120 East Van Buren
Phoenix, AZ 85004-2227

PAY SCALE: 0
WORD LENGTH: 800
COPYRIGHTED: yes
MUST LIVE IN AREA: yes
FREQUENCY: daily
PHONE NUMBER: 602-271-8477
FAX NUMBER: 602-271-8933

COMMENTS:

THE ARIZONA DAILY STAR
James M. Kiser, Editorial Page Editor
4850 South Park Avenue
Tucson, AZ 85714-3395

PAY SCALE: seldom
WORD LENGTH: 700-1,000
COPYRIGHTED: yes
MUST LIVE IN AREA: no
FREQUENCY: daily
PHONE NUMBER: 602-573-4235
FAX NUMBER: 602-573-4141

COMMENTS: Kiser prefers, "local topics especially. We rarely use out-of-state writers (other than syndicated columnists)." They pay "nothing—unless that's negotiated beforehand, and then usually no more than $35."

ARKANSAS

SOUTHWEST TIME RECORD

Debbye Hughes, City Editor
920 Rogers Avenue
Fort Smith, AR 72901-2696

PAY SCALE:
WORD LENGTH:
COPYRIGHTED:
MUST LIVE IN AREA:
FREQUENCY:
PHONE NUMBER: 501-785-7757
FAX NUMBER: 501-784-0413

COMMENTS: Hughes rarely uses freelance Op-Ed submissions, maybe four times per year.

ARKANSAS DEMOCRAT-GAZETTE

Meredith Oakley, Op-Ed Page Editor
P.O. Box 2221
Little Rock, AR 72203-2221

PAY SCALE:
WORD LENGTH:
COPYRIGHTED:
MUST LIVE IN AREA:
FREQUENCY:
PHONE NUMBER: 501-378-3400
FAX NUMBER: 501-372-3908

COMMENTS: They do not run any Op-Ed articles. They do, however, accept *Letters to the Editor*.

CALIFORNIA

BAKERSFIELD CALIFORNIAN

Diane Hardesty, Op-Ed Page Editor
1707 Eye Street
Bakersfield, CA 93301-5299

PAY SCALE: 0
WORD LENGTH: 750 for Viewpoint (Sun); 450 daily Op-Ed
COPYRIGHTED: no
MUST LIVE IN AREA: strong preference
FREQUENCY: daily
PHONE NUMBER: 805-395-7500
FAX NUMBER: 805-395-7519

COMMENTS: Hardesty wants submissions from local people on local topics. They do use some of the submissions for background for the Editorial Page. Sunday *Viewpoint* submissions should be authored by someone with credentials in the area they are writing about.

CONTRA COSTA TIMES

John Glenon, Op-Ed Page Editor
2640 Shadelands Drive
Contra Costa, CA 94598-2578

PAY SCALE: 0
WORD LENGTH: under 1,000
COPYRIGHTED: no
MUST LIVE IN AREA: no
FREQUENCY: Sun, Tues, Wed, Thurs, Fri.
PHONE NUMBER: 510-943-8253
FAX NUMBER: 510-943-8362

COMMENTS: Glenon prefers, "local issues primarily but will accept some others of general interest."

FRESNO BEE
Karen Baker, Editorial Page Editor
1626 E Street
Fresno, CA 93786-0001

PAY SCALE: $0-75
WORD LENGTH: 750
COPYRIGHTED: no, but if anything is reprinted the paper gets credit
MUST LIVE IN AREA: given priority
FREQUENCY: see comments
PHONE NUMBER: 209-441-6385
FAX NUMBER: 209-441-6436

COMMENTS: *Letters to the Editor* is run daily and three columns are run in *Valley Voices* on Saturday. Every six months the *Fresno Bee* hires five guest columnists to write one time a month for six months. Each earns $75 per month. They receive a large number of applications each time the positions open.

PRESS TELEGRAM
Larry Allison, Editorial Page Editor
604 Pine Avenue
Long Beach, CA 90844-0001

PAY SCALE: will pay on occasion
WORD LENGTH: 800 or less
COPYRIGHTED: yes
MUST LIVE IN AREA: preferred
FREQUENCY: daily
PHONE NUMBER: 310-435-1161
FAX NUMBER: 310-499-1277

COMMENTS: Interested in pieces on women's issues or local people dealing with global issues.

LOS ANGELES DAILY JOURNAL

Mark Thompson, Op-Ed Page Editor
P.O. Box 54026
Los Angeles, CA 90054

PAY SCALE: 0
WORD LENGTH: 500-2,000
COPYRIGHTED: yes
MUST LIVE IN AREA: no
FREQUENCY: daily
PHONE NUMBER: 213-229-5300
FAX NUMBER: 213-680-3682

COMMENTS: Thompson seeks articles on law.

LOS ANGELES TIMES

Robert A. Berger, Op-Ed Page Editor
Times Mirror Square
Los Angeles, CA 90053

PAY SCALE: $100-150
WORD LENGTH: 750
COPYRIGHTED: first time rights
MUST LIVE IN AREA: no
FREQUENCY: Sun-Fri
PHONE NUMBER: 213-237-7930
FAX NUMBER: 213-237-7968

COMMENTS:

MODESTO BEE
Dick LeGrand, Op-Ed Page Editor
1325 H Street
Modesto, CA 95354

PAY SCALE: nothing unless solicited, then tops would be $40
WORD LENGTH: 800
COPYRIGHTED: yes
MUST LIVE IN AREA: yes
FREQUENCY: daily
PHONE NUMBER: 209-578-2000
FAX NUMBER: 209-578-2207

COMMENTS: LeGrand doesn't specifically look for certain topics, it "depends on the course of the news." He prefers articles that are "focused" and "reflective of a real concern."

OAKLAND TRIBUNE
Robert C. Cuddy, Editorial Page Editor
409 13th Street
Oakland, CA 94612-2637

PAY SCALE: varies
WORD LENGTH: 500
COPYRIGHTED: yes
MUST LIVE IN AREA: no
FREQUENCY: daily
PHONE NUMBER: 510-416-4852
FAX NUMBER: 510-416-4850

COMMENTS: Cuddy seeks topics that are "not the usual stuff." Payment drops to $20 for multiple submissions. Reprint rights revert to author.

INLAND VALLEY DAILY BULLETIN
Kevin Chaffee, Op-Ed Page Editor
2041 East 4th Street
Ontario, CA 91764-2605

PAY SCALE: 0
WORD LENGTH: 750-1,000
COPYRIGHTED: yes
MUST LIVE IN AREA: prefer locally generated submissions
FREQUENCY: Sun
PHONE NUMBER: 909-987-6397
FAX NUMBER: 909-948-9038

COMMENTS: Chaffee will sometimes use freelance submissions on controversial state or local issues from credentialed individuals.

THE PRESS-ENTERPRISE
Joel Blain, Op-Ed Page Editor
3512 Fourteenth Street
Riverside, CA 92501-3878

PAY SCALE: $50
WORD LENGTH: 3-4 pages double-spaced
COPYRIGHTED: yes
MUST LIVE IN AREA: yes
FREQUENCY: Sun, The California Page
PHONE NUMBER: 909-684-1200
FAX NUMBER: 909-782-7572

COMMENTS:

THE SACRAMENTO BEE
Bill Kahrl, Opinion Editor
P.O. Box 15779
Sacramento, CA 95852

PAY SCALE: $150
WORD LENGTH: 750
COPYRIGHTED: no
MUST LIVE IN AREA: recommended
FREQUENCY: daily
PHONE NUMBER: 916-321-1000
FAX NUMBER: 916-321-1996

COMMENTS: Kahrl states, "In general, we're looking for good writing pieces that will make people think or provide a new insight into a familiar problem. We're especially interested in articles that treat local, state, or western regional issues. But that doesn't mean we wouldn't enjoy as well something that examines an aspect of our everyday lives, without the weight of public policy being figured in."

SALINAS CALIFORNIAN
Jim Albanese, Editorial Page Editor
P.O. Box 81091
Salinas, CA 93912-2644

PAY SCALE: 0
WORD LENGTH: 600
COPYRIGHTED: yes
MUST LIVE IN AREA: not necessarily, but prefers stories of local interest
FREQUENCY: Sat, editorials run daily
PHONE NUMBER: 408-424-2221
FAX NUMBER: 408-424-0117

COMMENTS:

SAN BERNADINO SUN
Richard Kimball, Op-Ed Page Editor
399 North D Street
San Bernadino, CA 92401-1581

PAY SCALE: 0
WORD LENGTH: 600
COPYRIGHTED: yes
MUST LIVE IN AREA: no, but prefer it
FREQUENCY: Sun
PHONE NUMBER: 909-889-9666
FAX NUMBER: 909-885-8741

COMMENTS: No specific topics are sought.

SAN DIEGO DAILY TRANSCRIPT
Andrew Kleske, City Editor
P.O. Box 85469
San Diego, CA 92138

PAY SCALE: 0
WORD LENGTH: 750-1,000
COPYRIGHTED: yes
MUST LIVE IN AREA: no
FREQUENCY: daily
PHONE NUMBER: 619-232-4381
FAX NUMBER: 619-236-8126

COMMENTS: Unless your submission is really "spectacular" you will not be paid. Also, if you're from outside the area, Kleske suggests you send an outline before spending a lot of time writing your essay.

THE SAN DIEGO UNION TRIBUNE
Bob Kittle, Editorial Page Editor
P.O. Box 191
San Diego, CA 92112-4106

PAY SCALE: $50-100
WORD LENGTH: 800
COPYRIGHTED: yes
MUST LIVE IN AREA: no
FREQUENCY: daily
PHONE NUMBER: 619-229-3131
FAX NUMBER: 619-293-1896

COMMENTS: Submit articles to the attention of Diane Clark.

SAN FRANCISCO CHRONICLE
Marsha VandeBerg, "Open Forum" Editor
901 Mission Street
San Francisco, CA 94103-2988

PAY SCALE: $100
WORD LENGTH: 650 or less
COPYRIGHTED: no
MUST LIVE IN AREA: no
FREQUENCY: daily
PHONE NUMBER: 415-777-7018
FAX NUMBER: 415-512-8196

COMMENTS: Looks for timeliness, writing ability, and topics of interest to a well-read, well-off readership. No satire or reminiscing. They prefer political or current comments.

SAN FRANCISCO EXAMINER
Jim Finefrock, Op-Ed Page Editor
110 Fifth Street
San Francisco, CA 94103-2972

PAY SCALE: $75
WORD LENGTH: 600
COPYRIGHTED: yes
MUST LIVE IN AREA: no
FREQUENCY: daily
PHONE NUMBER: 415-777-7923
FAX NUMBER: 415-777-1264

COMMENTS:

SAN JOSE MERCURY NEWS
Jim Braly, Op-Ed Page Editor
750 Ridder Park Drive
San Jose, CA 95190-0001

PAY SCALE: $50-75
WORD LENGTH: 750
COPYRIGHTED: yes
MUST LIVE IN AREA: no, but its easier. Locals are given preference
FREQUENCY: daily
PHONE NUMBER: 408-920-5000
FAX NUMBER: 408-288-8060

COMMENTS:

THE ORANGE COUNTY REGISTER

K. E. Grubbs, Jr., Editorial Page Editor
625 North Grand Avenue
Santa Ana, CA 92701-4347

PAY SCALE: $50
WORD LENGTH: 800
COPYRIGHTED: yes
MUST LIVE IN AREA: no
FREQUENCY: everyday but Saturday
PHONE NUMBER: 714-953-7980
FAX NUMBER: 714-565-3657

COMMENTS: The Sunday Commentary pays $100.

SANTA BARBARA NEWS-PRESS

John Lankford, Op-Ed Page Editor
P.O. Box 1359
Santa Barbara, CA 93102

PAY SCALE: 0
WORD LENGTH: 600-900
COPYRIGHTED: once published it's in the public domain
MUST LIVE IN AREA: preference to local writers, but depends on the subject
FREQUENCY: daily
PHONE NUMBER: 805-564-5200
FAX NUMBER: 805-966-6258

COMMENTS: Lankford prefers something topical or "responding to a hot issue." But that is by no means a requirement.

SANTA ROSA PRESS-DEMOCRAT
Pete Golis, Op-Ed Page Editor
427 Mendocino Avenue
Santa Rosa, CA 95401-6385

PAY SCALE: $50-100
WORD LENGTH: 750
COPYRIGHTED: yes
MUST LIVE IN AREA: no, but preferred
FREQUENCY: daily
PHONE NUMBER: 707-546-2020
FAX NUMBER: 707-546-8347

COMMENTS: Submit articles that focus on local issues.

THE DAILY BREEZE
Mike Carroll, Op-Ed Page Editor
5215 Torrance Boulevard
Torrance, CA 90509

PAY SCALE: $25
WORD LENGTH: 900
COPYRIGHTED: yes
MUST LIVE IN AREA: preferred
FREQUENCY: Sun-Fri
PHONE NUMBER: 310-540-5511
FAX NUMBER: 310-540-6272

COMMENTS: Carroll prefers submissions that concentrate more on local, regional issues.

DAILY NEWS
Mark Sims, Viewpoint/Opinions Editor
21221 Oxnard Street
Woodland Hills, CA 91367-5081

PAY SCALE: $75-150
WORD LENGTH: 750-900
COPYRIGHTED: yes
MUST LIVE IN AREA: no
FREQUENCY: daily
PHONE NUMBER: 818-713-3685
FAX NUMBER: 818-713-3723

COMMENTS:

COLORADO

COLORADO SPRINGS GAZETTE TELEGRAPH
Dan Griswold, Editorial Editor
30 South Prospect Street
Colorado Springs, CO 80903-3638

PAY SCALE:
WORD LENGTH:
COPYRIGHTED:
MUST LIVE IN AREA:
FREQUENCY:
PHONE NUMBER: 719-632-5511
FAX NUMBER: 719-636-0202

COMMENTS: They only use syndicated columnists.

THE DENVER POST
Bob Ewegen, Assistant Editor of Editorial Page
650 15th Street
Denver, CO 80201-5177

PAY SCALE: seldom
WORD LENGTH: 700-1,000
COPYRIGHTED: yes
MUST LIVE IN AREA: no
FREQUENCY: daily
PHONE NUMBER: 303-820-1010
FAX NUMBER: 303-820-1406

COMMENTS: They run 2-3 freelance submissions per week, usually arguing a cause or having an ax to grind. These they don't pay for. If they get a submission from a journalist who is writing something topical, they will pay a minimal sum of $35-50. Ewegen wants "stuff specific to Colorado" or the region. They use seven different wire services, so it has to be pretty good and a little unusual.

ROCKY MOUNTAIN NEWS
Vincent Carroll, Editorial Page Editor
400 West Colfax Avenue
Denver, CO 80204-2694

PAY SCALE: 0
WORD LENGTH: 600-750
COPYRIGHTED: yes
MUST LIVE IN AREA: no but Colorado writers given preference
FREQUENCY: 3 times a week
PHONE NUMBER: 303-892-5055
FAX NUMBER: 303-892-2658

COMMENTS: Send submissions to Jean Torkelson. Commentaries can be on various topics "as long as they're of interest to Colorado readers."

CONNECTICUT

CONNECTICUT POST
Stephen J. Winters, Op-Ed Page Editor
410 State Street
Bridgeport, CT 06604-4560

PAY SCALE: 0
WORD LENGTH: 3-4 double-spaced pages (or shorter)
COPYRIGHTED: yes
MUST LIVE IN AREA: no
FREQUENCY: daily
PHONE NUMBER: 203-330-6203
FAX NUMBER: 203-367-8158

COMMENTS: The paper "tends to concentrate on state and national issues—mostly politics." They pay only in exceptional cases and give preference to state writers.

HARTFORD COURANT
Elissa Papirno, Op-Ed Page Editor
285 Broad Street
Hartford, CT 06115-2510

PAY SCALE: 0
WORD LENGTH: 800
COPYRIGHTED: yes
MUST LIVE IN AREA: usually—we rarely use out of state freelance writers
FREQUENCY: daily
PHONE NUMBER: 203-241-6200
FAX NUMBER: 203-520-6927

COMMENTS:

NEW HAVEN REGISTER
Charles Kochakian, Editorial Page Editor
40 Sargent Drive
New Haven, CT 06511-5939

PAY SCALE: $50-100
WORD LENGTH: 750
COPYRIGHTED: no
MUST LIVE IN AREA: they are given preference
FREQUENCY: depends on room available
PHONE NUMBER: 203-789-5200
FAX NUMBER: 203-865-7894

COMMENTS: Kochakian currently has more freelance submissions than he knows what to do with.

STAMFORD ADVOCATE
Deirdre Channing, Editorial Page Editor
75 Tresser Boulevard
Stamford, CT 06901-3300

PAY SCALE:
WORD LENGTH:
COPYRIGHTED:
MUST LIVE IN AREA:
FREQUENCY:
PHONE NUMBER: 203-964-2200
FAX NUMBER: 203-964-2345

COMMENTS: They do not use any freelance for their Opinion Page. However, they do accept freelance for their Editorial Page but it does not pay.

WATERBURY REPUBLICAN-AMERICAN

Connie LePore, Op-Ed Page Editor
389 Meadow Street
Waterbury, CT 06702-1898

PAY SCALE: $40
WORD LENGTH: 18-22 inches
COPYRIGHTED: yes
MUST LIVE IN AREA: no
FREQUENCY: 3 times per week
PHONE NUMBER: 203-574-3636 ext 340
FAX NUMBER: 203-596-9277

COMMENTS: LePore comments, "You'd be competing against our syndicated columnists, who get paid even if we don't use their pieces."

DELAWARE

NEWS-JOURNAL
John H. Taylor, Jr., Op-Ed Page Editor
950 West Basin Road
New Castle, DE 19720

PAY SCALE: seldom, then very little
WORD LENGTH: 500-600
COPYRIGHTED: first-time rights
MUST LIVE IN AREA: yes
FREQUENCY: daily except Sat
PHONE NUMBER: 302-324-2500
FAX NUMBER: 302-324-2595

COMMENTS:

FLORIDA

DAYTONA BEACH NEWS-JOURNAL
Lee Moore, Op-Ed Page Editor
901 Sixth Street
Daytona Beach, FL 32117-8099

PAY SCALE: 0
WORD LENGTH: 250-300
COPYRIGHTED: yes
MUST LIVE IN AREA: no
FREQUENCY: daily
PHONE NUMBER: 904-252-1511
FAX NUMBER: 904-258-8465

COMMENTS: Lee uses freelance submissions from experts in their field with education or business credentials. He prefers current topics.

SUN SENTINEL
Kingsley Guy, Editorial Page Editor
200 East Las Olas Boulevard
Fort Lauderdale, FL 33301-2293

PAY SCALE: 0
WORD LENGTH: 2½ pages double-spaced
COPYRIGHTED: yes
MUST LIVE IN AREA: no
FREQUENCY: daily
PHONE NUMBER: 305-356-4000
FAX NUMBER: 305-356-4559

COMMENTS: Freelance articles should be submitted to the Assistant Editorial Page Editor, Robin Branch. If you are out of the area, please make sure you include telephone numbers where you can be reached.

THE NEWS-PRESS
Homer Pyle, Op-Ed Page Editor
2442 Martin Luther King Junior Blvd.
Ft. Myers, FL 33901

PAY SCALE: 0
WORD LENGTH: 800
COPYRIGHTED: yes
MUST LIVE IN AREA: no
FREQUENCY: daily
PHONE NUMBER: 813-335-0224
FAX NUMBER: 813-334-0708

COMMENTS:

FLORIDA TIMES-UNION
Lloyd Brown, Op-Ed Page Editor
P.O. Box 1949
Jacksonville, FL 32231

PAY SCALE: 0
WORD LENGTH: 600-700
COPYRIGHTED: yes
MUST LIVE IN AREA: no, but given strong preference
FREQUENCY: daily
PHONE NUMBER: 904-359-4111
FAX NUMBER: 904-359-4478

COMMENTS: Most of the Op-Ed page is filled by syndicated columnists. If there is room, they will use a local writer who has chosen a pertinent topic.

MIAMI HERALD

Martha Musgrove, Op-Ed Page Editor
One Herald Plaza
Miami, FL 33132-1693

PAY SCALE: 0
WORD LENGTH: 700
COPYRIGHTED: yes
MUST LIVE IN AREA: no
FREQUENCY: daily
PHONE NUMBER: 305-350-2111
FAX NUMBER: 305-376-2072

COMMENTS: Prefers submissions on local issues.

ORLANDO SENTINEL

Mike Murphy, Op-Ed Page Editor
633 North Orange Avenue
Orlando, FL 32801-1349

PAY SCALE: varies
WORD LENGTH: 650-700
COPYRIGHTED: no
MUST LIVE IN AREA: no, but given preference
FREQUENCY: daily
PHONE NUMBER: 407-420-5168
FAX NUMBER: 407-420-5286

COMMENTS: My Word, the daily Op-Ed section, is done on a gratis basis.

SARASOTA HERALD-TRIBUNE
Thomas Lee Tryon, Editorial Page Editor
801 South Tamiami Trail
Sarasota, FL 34236

PAY SCALE: 0
WORD LENGTH: 800
COPYRIGHTED: yes
MUST LIVE IN AREA: no
FREQUENCY: daily
PHONE NUMBER: 813-957-5225
FAX NUMBER: 813-957-5276

COMMENTS:

ST. PETERSBURG TIMES
Philip L. Gailey, Op-Ed Page Editor
490 First Avenue South
St. Petersburg, FL 33701

PAY SCALE: $150-300
WORD LENGTH: 800
COPYRIGHTED: yes
MUST LIVE IN AREA: no
FREQUENCY: daily
PHONE NUMBER: 813-893-8268
FAX NUMBER: 813-893-8675

COMMENTS:

TAMPA TRIBUNE
Nancy Gordon, Op-Ed Page Editor
202 South Parker Street
Tampa, FL 33606-2395

PAY SCALE: $100
WORD LENGTH: 600-800
COPYRIGHTED: yes
MUST LIVE IN AREA: no
FREQUENCY: daily, including Sunday Commentary
PHONE NUMBER: 813-259-7775
FAX NUMBER: 813-259-7676

COMMENTS: Gordon states topics sought are, "those on which you have special expertise or a unique viewpoint. Avoid redundancy of mainstream syndicated columnists." They do purchase at $100, but usually only if they are suitable for the cover page Sunday display.

VERO BEACH PRESS JOURNAL
Larry Reisman, Op-Ed Page Editor
1801 US Highway 1
Vero Beach, FL 32960-0997

PAY SCALE: 0
WORD LENGTH: 800-1,000
COPYRIGHTED: no
MUST LIVE IN AREA: no
FREQUENCY: daily
PHONE NUMBER: 407-562-2315
FAX NUMBER: 407-562-7210

COMMENTS: Reisman prefers topics "on Florida or Indian River County issues."

PALM BEACH POST
Randy Schultz, Op-Ed Page Editor
2751 South Dixie Highway
West Palm Beach, FL 33405-1298

PAY SCALE: 0
WORD LENGTH: it depends on the topic
COPYRIGHTED: no
MUST LIVE IN AREA: no
FREQUENCY: daily
PHONE NUMBER: 407-820-4471
FAX NUMBER: 407-820-4728

COMMENTS: You don't have to live in the area to submit, but they do prefer topics that have a local appeal.

GEORGIA

ATLANTA CONSTITUTION
N.V. Raman, Op-Ed Page Editor
P.O. Box 4689
Atlanta, GA 30302-2804

PAY SCALE: 0
WORD LENGTH: 600
COPYRIGHTED: yes
MUST LIVE IN AREA: no
FREQUENCY: daily
PHONE NUMBER: 404-526-5377
FAX NUMBER: 404-526-5611

COMMENTS:

ATLANTA JOURNAL
James Wooten, Editorial Page Editor
72 Marietta Street, NW
Atlanta, GA 30303-2804

PAY SCALE: 0
WORD LENGTH: 500
COPYRIGHTED: yes
MUST LIVE IN AREA: no, but they are given strong preference
FREQUENCY: daily
PHONE NUMBER: 404-526-5151
FAX NUMBER: 404-526-5746

COMMENTS: Wooten prefers topical subjects, sometimes humorous.

AUGUSTA CHRONICLE/AUGUSTA HERALD

Philip A. Kent, Op-Ed Page Editor
725 Broad Street
Augusta, GA 30901-1305

PAY SCALE: 0
WORD LENGTH: 2 pages double-spaced
COPYRIGHTED: yes
MUST LIVE IN AREA: yes
FREQUENCY: daily
PHONE NUMBER: 706-724-0851
FAX NUMBER: 706-722-7403

COMMENTS: They rarely use freelance submissions. Their Op-Ed page has a lot of advertising and first priority goes to syndicated columnists. They use topical issues that are state or local from credentialed experts. Include a picture with your submission.

MACON TELEGRAPH

Ed Carson, Op-Ed Page Editor
120 Broadway
Macon, GA 31201-3444

PAY SCALE: $15
WORD LENGTH: 600
COPYRIGHTED: yes
MUST LIVE IN AREA: yes
FREQUENCY: daily
PHONE NUMBER: 912-744-4200
FAX NUMBER: 912-744-4385

COMMENTS: Carson doesn't use much freelance for Op-Eds. He has syndicated columnists and uses local writers. Most of their freelance comes in the form of *Letters to the Editor*.

HAWAII

HONOLULU ADVERTISER
Jerry Burris, Op-Ed Page Editor
605 Kapiolani Boulevard
Honolulu, HI 96813-5129

PAY SCALE:
WORD LENGTH:
COPYRIGHTED:
MUST LIVE IN AREA:
FREQUENCY:
PHONE NUMBER:
FAX NUMBER:

COMMENTS: Burris states, "I'm sorry—not in market at this time. Aloha."

HONOLULU STAR-BULLETIN
Diane Chang, Editorial Page Editor
605 Kapiolani Boulevard
Honolulu, HI 96813-5129

PAY SCALE: 0, unless solicited
WORD LENGTH: 800-1,000 (prefers 800)
COPYRIGHTED: no
MUST LIVE IN AREA: yes, use mainly local writers
FREQUENCY: Fri, Mon
PHONE NUMBER: 808-525-8607
FAX NUMBER: 808-523-8409

COMMENTS:

IDAHO

THE IDAHO STATESMAN
Michelle Cole, Metro Editor
1200 North Curtis Road
Boise, ID 83706-1239

PAY SCALE: 0
WORD LENGTH: 450-500
COPYRIGHTED: yes
MUST LIVE IN AREA: yes
FREQUENCY: Sunday
PHONE NUMBER: 208-377-6432
FAX NUMBER: 208-377-6449

COMMENTS: They prefer issues related to Boise.

IDAHO FALLS POST REGISTER
Gene Fadness, Editorial Page Editor
333 Northgate Mile
Idaho Falls, ID 83401-2529

PAY SCALE: 0
WORD LENGTH: 300 or less
COPYRIGHTED: no
MUST LIVE IN AREA: no
FREQUENCY: daily
PHONE NUMBER: 208-522-1800
FAX NUMBER: 208-529-3142

COMMENTS: The shorter the submission, the less likely it is to be edited.

ILLINOIS

CHAMPAIGN NEWS GAZETTE
Rosemary Garhart, Editorial Page Editor
15 Main Street
Champaign, IL 61820-0677

PAY SCALE: 0
WORD LENGTH: 800-1,000
COPYRIGHTED: yes
MUST LIVE IN AREA: preferred, but not required
FREQUENCY: weekly
PHONE NUMBER: 217-351-5381
FAX NUMBER: 217-351-5374

COMMENTS: Topics sought are local and state issues.

CHICAGO SUN TIMES
Mark Hornung, Op-Ed Page Editor
401 North Wabash Avenue
Chicago, IL 60611-3593

PAY SCALE: 0
WORD LENGTH: doesn't matter, they'll edit
COPYRIGHTED: first-time rights
MUST LIVE IN AREA: yes
FREQUENCY: daily
PHONE NUMBER: 312-321-2510
FAX NUMBER: 312-321-2120

COMMENTS:

CHICAGO TRIBUNE
Dianne Donovan, Op-Ed Page Editor
435 North Michigan Avenue
Chicago, IL 60611-4041

PAY SCALE:
WORD LENGTH:
COPYRIGHTED:
MUST LIVE IN AREA:
FREQUENCY:
PONE NUMBER: 312-222-4594
FAX NUMBER: 312-222-3143

COMMENTS: They would not discuss freelance submissions over the phone or via fax.

PEORIA JOURNAL-STAR
Barbara Mantz Drake, Op-Ed Page Editor
One News Plaza
Peoria, IL 61643-0002

PAY SCALE: $40-75
WORD LENGTH: 600-700
COPYRIGHTED: yes
MUST LIVE IN AREA: no, but preferred
FREQUENCY: Sundays only
PHONE NUMBER: 309-686-3133
FAX NUMBER: 309-686-3296

COMMENTS:

INDIANA

EVANSVILLE COURIER

Chuck Leach, Op-Ed Page Editor
300 East Walnut
Evansville, IN 47713-1938

PAY SCALE: 0
WORD LENGTH: no more than 3 pages
COPYRIGHTED: yes
MUST LIVE IN AREA: yes
FREQUENCY: daily
PHONE NUMBER: 812-464-7415
FAX NUMBER: 812-422-8196

COMMENTS: Leach wants "any topic as long as it's tied to something local."

INDIANAPOLIS NEWS

Russ Pulliam, Op-Ed Page Editor
307 North Pennsylvania Street
Indianapolis, IN 46204-1811

PAY SCALE: Negotiable, generally nothing unless solicited
WORD LENGTH: 700-800
COPYRIGHTED: yes
MUST LIVE IN AREA: yes—there are exceptions however
FREQUENCY: daily
PHONE NUMBER: 317-633-1240
FAX NUMBER: 317-633-1038

COMMENTS:

INDIANAPOLIS STAR
John Lyst, Op-Ed Page Editor
P.O. Box 145
Indianapolis, IN 46206-0145

PAY SCALE: $40
WORD LENGTH: 650-800
COPYRIGHTED: yes
MUST LIVE IN AREA: no
FREQUENCY: daily
PHONE NUMBER: 317-633-1240
FAX NUMBER: 317-633-9423

COMMENTS:

SOUTH BEND TRIBUNE
Margaret Fosmore, Op-Ed Page Editor
225 West Colfax Avenue
South Bend, IN 46626-1001

PAY SCALE: 0
WORD LENGTH: 500-800
COPYRIGHTED: yes
MUST LIVE IN AREA: no, but must relate back to the area
FREQUENCY: Mon-Fri
PHONE NUMBER: 219-235-6161
FAX NUMBER: 219-236-1765

COMMENTS: "Michiana Point of View" runs five days per week. Also, you can submit *Letters to the Editor*, which they prefer be 200 words.

IOWA

CEDAR RAPIDS GAZETTE

Jerry Elsea, Editorial Page Editor
500 Third Avenue, SE
Cedar Rapids, IA 52401-1608

PAY SCALE: $20
WORD LENGTH: 750
COPYRIGHTED: up to author—not usually
MUST LIVE IN AREA: yes
FREQUENCY: Opinion Page—daily, 2nd Opinion—Thurs, Sun
PHONE NUMBER: 319-398-8262
FAX NUMBER: 319-398-5846

COMMENTS: Elsea prefers you "live in the area." They use very little outside freelance material.

DES MOINES REGISTER

Dennis Ryerson, Editorial Page Editor
715 Locust Street
Des Moines, IA 50309-0957

PAY SCALE: $25-100
WORD LENGTH: 500-850
COPYRIGHTED: first-time rights only
MUST LIVE IN AREA: yes
FREQUENCY: daily
PHONE NUMBER: 515-284-8000
FAX NUMBER: 515-286-2504

COMMENTS: Ryerson's Editorial Assistant states, "a postcard will be sent within a week to ten days if we intend to use your piece. If you would like to have your unused piece returned to you, you need to include a stamped self-addressed envelope. Standard payment is $25-50 for average size pieces and $75-100 for longer Sunday Forum pieces. The *Des Moines Register* has first-time rights only. After it has been published in our paper, the writer may submit it anywhere they wish."

SIOUX CITY JOURNAL
Larry Myhre, Op-Ed Page Editor
515 Pavonia Street, Box 118
Sioux City, IA 51102

PAY SCALE:
WORD LENGTH:
COPYRIGHTED:
MUST LIVE IN AREA:
FREQUENCY:
PHONE NUMBER:
FAX NUMBER:

COMMENTS: Myhre says, "Sorry, we do not currently have a need for this service."

KANSAS

TOPEKA CAPITAL-JOURNAL
Michael Ryan, Editorial Page Editor
616 SE Jefferson
Topeka, KS 66607

PAY SCALE: 0
WORD LENGTH: 500-600
COPYRIGHTED: yes
MUST LIVE IN AREA: generally
FREQUENCY: Sunday
PHONE NUMBER: 913-295-1111
FAX NUMBER: 913-295-1230

COMMENTS:

WICHITA EAGLE
Shannon Littlejohn, Op-Ed Page Editor
P.O. Box 820
Wichita, KS 67201-3594

PAY SCALE: $50-75
WORD LENGTH: 800
COPYRIGHTED: yes
MUST LIVE IN AREA: yes, mostly
FREQUENCY: daily
PHONE NUMBER: 316-268-6367
FAX NUMBER: 316-268-6627

COMMENTS: Prefer topics on local issues.

KENTUCKY

THE KENTUCKY POST
Shirl Short, Op-Ed Page Editor
421 Madison Avenue
Covington, KY 41011

PAY SCALE: 0
WORD LENGTH: 500-600
COPYRIGHTED: yes
MUST LIVE IN AREA: no
FREQUENCY: once a week
PHONE NUMBER: 606-292-2616
FAX NUMBER: 606-291-2525

COMMENTS: Short comments, "Once a week we devote the editorial page to one theme or issue. Our emphasis is local/state issues."

LEXINGTON HERALD-LEADER
Art Jester, Op-Ed Page Editor
100 Midland Avenue
Lexington, KY 40508-1999

PAY SCALE: seldom
WORD LENGTH: 650
COPYRIGHTED: first time rights
MUST LIVE IN AREA: yes
FREQUENCY: 3-4 times per week
PHONE NUMBER: 606-231-3200
FAX NUMBER: 606-254-9738

COMMENTS: Jester does not use essays from out of state. They "have a snowballs chance in hell." He uses local and state authors who write about local and state issues.

THE COURIER-JOURNAL
Keith Runyan, Op-Ed Page Editor
525 West Broadway
Louisville, KY 40202-2137

PAY SCALE: 0
WORD LENGTH: 700
COPYRIGHTED: yes
MUST LIVE IN AREA: no
FREQUENCY: 5 days a week
PHONE NUMBER: 502-582-4594
FAX NUMBER: 502-582-4066

COMMENTS:

LOUISIANA

THE ADVOCATE
John LaPlante, Op-Ed Page Editor
525 Lafayette Street
Baton Rouge, LA 70802-5410

PAY SCALE:
WORD LENGTH:
COPYRIGHTED:
MUST LIVE IN AREA:
FREQUENCY:
PHONE NUMBER: 504-383-1111
FAX NUMBER: 504-383-0371

COMMENTS: They accept no Op-Ed freelance submissions, it's all written by syndicated columnists. You can however submit *Letters to the Editor.*

LAKE CHARLES AMERICAN PRESS
Bobby Dower, Op-Ed Page Editor
4900 East Highway 90
Lake Charles, LA 70602

PAY SCALE: 0
WORD LENGTH: maximum two pages double-spaced
COPYRIGHTED: no
MUST LIVE IN AREA: most of the time
FREQUENCY: Sundays
PHONE NUMBER: 318-433-3000
FAX NUMBER: 318-494-4070

COMMENTS:

TIMES-PICAYUNE
Malcolm Forsyth, Op-Ed Page Editor
3800 Howard Avenue
New Orleans, LA 71040

PAY SCALE:
WORD LENGTH:
COPYRIGHTED:
MUST LIVE IN AREA:
FREQUENCY:
PHONE NUMBER: 504-826-3279
FAX NUMBER: 504-826-3007

COMMENTS: Forsyth accepts no freelance Op-Ed submissions, he solicits writers.

THE TIMES
Frank May, Editorial Page Editor
222 Lake Street
Shreveport, LA 71101-3799

PAY SCALE: 0
WORD LENGTH: 600-800
COPYRIGHTED: yes
MUST LIVE IN AREA: yes
FREQUENCY: about every other day
PHONE NUMBER: 318-459-3200
FAX NUMBER: 318-459-3301

COMMENTS: Please send a picture with your submission and include a tag line.

MAINE

PORTLAND PRESS HERALD
Michael D. Harmon, Op-Ed Page Editor
390 Congress Street
Portland, ME 04101-1103

PAY SCALE: 0
WORD LENGTH: 750-800
COPYRIGHTED: first time rights
MUST LIVE IN AREA: yes
FREQUENCY: daily
PHONE NUMBER: 207-780-9000
IN MAINE: 800-442-6036
FAX NUMBER:

COMMENTS: Michael is looking for state and state issue submissions. He would also like to find an expert to write a column, Maine Voices, appearing 2-3 times per week.

MARYLAND

THE BALTIMORE SUN
Harold D. Piper, Opinion-Commentary Page
501 North Calvert Street
Baltimore, MD 21278-0001

PAY SCALE: $100 for articles, $50 for poetry, $50 for art
WORD LENGTH: 800
COPYRIGHTED: yes, unless rights are requested by the author
MUST LIVE IN AREA: no, but it helps
FREQUENCY: daily, except Saturday
PHONE NUMBER: 410-332-6053
FAX NUMBER: 410-752-6049

COMMENTS: Piper indicates "about a third of our material comes from freelancers. The page is not a talk show where any idiot is entitled to sound off, we have *Letters to the Editor* for that. The Op-Ed page should be informative, literate and readable." It can sometimes take up to three months for a reply; the delay usually means your article is being considered. Include your Social Security Number and some brief bio material. They also request a self-addressed, stamped envelope or a reply card.

FREDERICK POST
Michael Powell, Editorial Page Editor
P.O. Box 578
Frederick, MD 21701

PAY SCALE:
WORD LENGTH:
COPYRIGHTED:
MUST LIVE IN AREA:
FREQUENCY:
PHONE NUMBER: 301-662-1177
FAX NUMBER: 301-662-8299

COMMENTS: Refused to respond to numerous phone and fax inquires.

MASSACHUSETTS

THE BOSTON GLOBE
Marjorie Pritchard, Op-Ed Page Editor
135 Morrissey Boulevard
Boston, MA 02107-2378

PAY SCALE: $150
WORD LENGTH: 700
COPYRIGHTED: first time rights
MUST LIVE IN AREA: no
FREQUENCY: daily
PHONE NUMBER: 617-929-3041
FAX NUMBER: 617-929-2098

COMMENTS: Wants topics in the news. Favors submissions from New Englanders.

THE BOSTON HERALD
Rachelle G. Cohen, Op-Ed Page Editor
One Herald Square
Boston, MA 02106-2096

PAY SCALE: $75-150
WORD LENGTH: 600-800
COPYRIGHTED: yes
MUST LIVE IN AREA: yes
FREQUENCY: daily
PHONE NUMBER: 617-426-3000
FAX NUMBER: 617-426-1865

COMMENTS:

SPRINGFIELD UNION-NEWS
Joseph Hopkins, Op-Ed Page Editor
P.O. Box 15012
Springfield, MA 01101

PAY SCALE: 0
WORD LENGTH: 750-800
COPYRIGHTED: no, but will not run articles that appear elsewhere
MUST LIVE IN AREA: yes
FREQUENCY: daily
PHONE NUMBER: 413-788-1200
FAX NUMBER: 413-788-1301

COMMENTS: Hopkins runs three syndicated columns each day and puts in Op-Ed submissions on the right-hand side of the paper. With each submission they like to run a head and shoulders picture with a brief biography listing credentials. In December of 1994 they will be rearranging the column, allowing more space for freelance submissions.

WORCESTER TELEGRAM & GAZETTE
Robert Nemeth, Editorial Page Editor
20 Franklin Street
Worcester, MA 01615-0012

PAY SCALE: 0
WORD LENGTH: 3 pages, double-spaced
COPYRIGHTED: no
MUST LIVE IN AREA: yes
FREQUENCY: daily
PHONE NUMBER: 508-793-9100
FAX NUMBER: 508-793-9281

COMMENT: A daily section, As I See It, is reserved for comments from credentialed writers.

MICHIGAN

DETROIT FREE PRESS
William Rapai, Op-Ed Page Editor
321 West Lafayette
Detroit, MI 48226-2706

PAY SCALE: $50-200
WORD LENGTH: 800
COPYRIGHTED: yes
MUST LIVE IN AREA: no, but given priority
FREQUENCY: Sun-Fri
PHONE NUMBER: 313-222-6583
FAX NUMBER: 313-222-6774

COMMENTS:

THE DETROIT NEWS
Thomas J. Bray, Op-Ed Page Editor
615 West Lafayette Boulevard
Detroit, MI 48226-3197

PAY SCALE: $75
WORD LENGTH: 500-750
COPYRIGHTED: yes
MUST LIVE IN AREA: no
FREQUENCY: daily
PHONE NUMBER: 313-222-2297
FAX NUMBER: 313-222-6417

COMMENTS: Bray indicates, "first priority is given to articles on subjects of local or state interest."

THE FLINT JOURNAL

David J. Fenech, Op-Ed Page Editor
200 East First Street
Flint, MI 48502

PAY SCALE: 0
WORD LENGTH: none indicated
COPYRIGHTED: yes
MUST LIVE IN AREA: generally yes
FREQUENCY: Sun-Fri
PHONE NUMBER: 810-766-6189
FAX NUMBER: 810-767-7518

COMMENTS: They do accept articles from outside the area if you're writing something specific about Flint.

LANSING STATE JOURNAL

Mark Nixon, Editorial Page Editor
120 E. Lenewee Street
Lansing, MI 48919-0001

PAY SCALE: 0
WORD LENGTH: 600
COPYRIGHTED: yes
MUST LIVE IN AREA: yes
FREQUENCY: daily
PHONE NUMBER: 517-377-1000
FAX NUMBER: 517-377-1298

COMMENTS: Nixon likes "input from readers" of general interest.

MINNESOTA

STAR TRIBUNE

Eric Ringham, Commentary Editor
425 Portland Avenue, South
Minneapolis, MN 55488-0002

PAY SCALE: $100
WORD LENGTH: 800 or less
COPYRIGHTED: yes
MUST LIVE IN AREA: yes
FREQUENCY: daily
PHONE NUMBER: 612-673-4000
FAX NUMBER: 612-673-4359

COMMENTS: Send submissions to "Commentary."

ST. PAUL PIONEER PRESS

Steve Dornfeld, Op-Ed Page Editor
345 Cedar Street
St. Paul, MN 55101-1057

PAY SCALE: $75
WORD LENGTH: 700-750
COPYRIGHTED: yes
MUST LIVE IN AREA: yes
FREQUENCY: daily
PHONE NUMBER: 612-228-5427
FAX NUMBER: 612-222-6129

COMMENTS: Dornfeld prefers "issues of local relevance."

MISSISSIPPI

BILOXI-GULFPORT SUN HERALD
Marie Harris, Op-Ed Page Editor
P.O. Box 4567
Biloxi, MS 39535-4567

PAY SCALE: 0
WORD LENGTH: 700-900
COPYRIGHTED: yes
MUST LIVE IN AREA: no
FREQUENCY: daily
PHONE NUMBER: 601-896-2301
FAX NUMBER: 601-896-2104

COMMENTS:

JACKSON CLARION-LEDGER
David Hampton, Op-Ed Page Editor
311 East Pearl Street
Jackson, MS 39201-3499

PAY SCALE: varies
WORD LENGTH: 700
COPYRIGHTED: yes
MUST LIVE IN AREA: yes
FREQUENCY: daily
PHONE NUMBER: 601-961-7242
FAX NUMBER: 601-961-7211

COMMENTS:

MISSOURI

KANSAS CITY STAR
Virginia Hall, Op-Ed Page Editor
1729 Grand Avenue
Kansas City, MO 64108-1458

PAY SCALE: $75-200
WORD LENGTH: 800-1,000
COPYRIGHTED: yes
MUST LIVE IN AREA: no
FREQUENCY: daily
PHONE NUMBER: 816-234-4141
FAX NUMBER: 816-234-4926

COMMENTS: They would like to see newsworthy items.

THE NEWS-LEADER
George Freeman, Op-Ed Page Editor
651 Boonville Avenue
Springfield, MO 65806-1005

PAY SCALE: 0
WORD LENGTH: 500-600
COPYRIGHTED: yes
MUST LIVE IN AREA: yes
FREQUENCY: Sun, Mon
PHONE NUMBER: 417-836-1100
FAX NUMBER: 417-837-1381

COMMENTS: Freeman is flooded with submissions from one local university and three colleges. Make it brief and establish a local connection. Articles can be submitted through InfoNet. Freeman is very helpful on the phone.

ST. LOUIS POST-DISPATCH

Donna Korando, Op-Ed Page Editor
900 North Tucker Boulevard
St. Louis, MO 63101-1099

PAY SCALE: $70
WORD LENGTH: 750
COPYRIGHTED: yes, but only first time rights
MUST LIVE IN AREA: greatly prefer
FREQUENCY: 6 days
PHONE NUMBER: 314-340-8000
FAX NUMBER: 314-340-3050

COMMENTS: Open to any topics.

MONTANA

MONTANA STANDARD
Jeff Gibson, Editorial Page Editor
25 West Granite
Butte, MT 59701-9213

PAY SCALE:
WORD LENGTH:
COPYRIGHTED:
MUST LIVE IN AREA:
FREQUENCY:
PHONE NUMBER:
FAX NUMBER:

COMMENTS: Gibson states, "don't have Op-Ed page, rarely use stuff outside this circulation area—pays nothing."

GREAT FALLS TRIBUNE
Eric Newhouse, Editorial Page Editor
P.O. Box 5468
Great Falls, MT 59403

PAY SCALE: 0
WORD LENGTH: depends on subject
COPYRIGHTED: yes
MUST LIVE IN AREA: yes
FREQUENCY:
PHONE NUMBER: 406-761-6666
FAX NUMBER: 406-791-1431

COMMENTS: *The Tribune* uses nationally syndicated columnists for the news of the world, but relies on the citizens of Montana for a "better state view." They receive such a large volume of letters each year that unless you're from the area, don't bother.

NEBRASKA

LINCOLN STAR
Nancy Hicks, Editorial Page Editor
926 P Street
Lincoln, NE 68508-3615

PAY SCALE: 0
WORD LENGTH: depends on area of submission
COPYRIGHTED: first time rights
MUST LIVE IN AREA: yes
FREQUENCY: daily
PHONE NUMBER: 402-475-4200
FAX NUMBER: 402-473-7291

COMMENTS: There are three ways to submit articles: Letters to the Editor, Point of View, and Reader Columns. The first two do not pay and should be shorter in length. The Reader Columns are done by invitation, run for two Saturdays, and are paid at $25 per column. To submit your name for consideration, contact Kate Gaul.

OMAHA WORLD HERALD
Frank Partsch, Op-Ed Page Editor
World Herald Square
Omaha, NE 68102

PAY SCALE: $20 and up
WORD LENGTH: 600-700
COPYRIGHTED: yes
MUST LIVE IN AREA: no
FREQUENCY: daily
PHONE NUMBER: 402-444-2366
FAX NUMBER: 402-345-4547

COMMENTS: You can also contact Larry Novicki the Editorial Page Coordinator at ext 2367. They rarely use freelance material from outside the area; however, Nebraska, Western Iowa, Kansas, North East Colorado, Wyoming, and South Dakota are in their circulation area due to the old train routes. Yes, you read right!

NEVADA

LAS VEGAS REVIEW-JOURNAL
John Kerr, Op-Ed Page Editor
1111 West Bonanza Boulevard
Las Vegas, NV 89106-3545

PAY SCALE: 0
WORD LENGTH: 750
COPYRIGHTED: first time rights
MUST LIVE IN AREA: preferred
FREQUENCY: daily
PHONE NUMBER: 702-383-0211
FAX NUMBER: 702-383-0302

COMMENTS: Kerr prefers articles that are "tailored to the area."

LAS VEGAS SUN
Larry Wills, Editorial Page Editor
800 South Valley View Boulevard
Las Vegas, NV 89107

PAY SCALE: 0
WORD LENGTH: 2 pages double-spaced
COPYRIGHTED: first time rights
MUST LIVE IN AREA: preferred
FREQUENCY: daily
PHONE NUMBER: 702-385-3111
FAX NUMBER: 702-383-7264

COMMENTS: Wills prefers articles that focus on Las Vegas and the Southwest, he relies on syndicated columnists to cover the national issues.

RENO GAZETTE JOURNAL
Bruce Bledsoe, Op-Ed Page Editor
955 Kuenzli Street
Reno, NV 89502-1160

PAY SCALE: 0
WORD LENGTH: 500
COPYRIGHTED: yes
MUST LIVE IN AREA: preferred
FREQUENCY: Sun
PHONE NUMBER: 702-788-6200
FAX NUMBER: 702-788-6458

COMMENTS:

NEW HAMPSHIRE

FOSTER'S DAILY DEMOCRAT
Philip Kincade, Editorial Page Editor
333 Central Avenue
Dover, NH 03820-4170

PAY SCALE: 0
WORD LENGTH: 300
COPYRIGHTED: yes
MUST LIVE IN AREA: yes
FREQUENCY: daily
PHONE NUMBER: 603-742-4455
FAX NUMBER: 603-749-4029

COMMENTS: Submissions can be made in the form of *Letters to the Editor*.

THE UNION LEADER
James Finnegan, Editorial Page Editor
100 William Loeb Drive
Manchester, NH 03108-9555

PAY SCALE:
WORD LENGTH:
COPYRIGHTED:
MUST LIVE IN AREA:
FREQUENCY:
PHONE NUMBER: 603-668-4321
FAX NUMBER: 603-668-0382

COMMENTS: Finnegan uses his regular columnists for most pieces on the Op-Ed page. You can submit unsolicited material but he won't guarantee anything.

NEW JERSEY

THE RECORD
Roy Graham, Op-Ed Page Editor
150 River Street
Hackensack, NJ 07601-7155

PAY SCALE: $50-200
WORD LENGTH: 1,000 for daily, 800 for Sunday
COPYRIGHTED: yes
MUST LIVE IN AREA: preferred
FREQUENCY: daily
PHONE NUMBER: 609-663-6000
FAX NUMBER: 609-663-2831

COMMENTS: Graham uses the wire service to cover national issues so he prefers that articles submitted be from "local writers" about "state wide issues."

JERSEY JOURNAL
Robert Larkins, Op-Ed Page Editor
30 Journal Square
Jersey City, NJ 07306-4199

PAY SCALE: 0
WORD LENGTH: 400 or less
COPYRIGHTED: won't print previously published material
MUST LIVE IN AREA: strongly encouraged
FREQUENCY: Irregular schedule, set by production
PHONE NUMBER: 201-217-2402
FAX NUMBER: 201-653-1414

COMMENTS:

THE STAR LEDGER
Robert Kalter, Op-Ed Page Editor
1 Star Ledger Plaza
Newark, NJ 07101

PAY SCALE:
WORD LENGTH:
COPYRIGHTED:
MUST LIVE IN AREA:
FREQUENCY:
PHONE NUMBER:
FAX NUMBER:

COMMENTS: They use only staff-generated or syndicate-supplied columns.

NORTH JERSEY HERALD
Kenneth G. Pringle, Editorial Page Editor
988 Main Avenue
Passaic, NJ 07055-8619

PAY SCALE: "zilch"
WORD LENGTH: 500 maximum
COPYRIGHTED: yes
MUST LIVE IN AREA: no
FREQUENCY: Sunday
PHONE NUMBER: 201-365-3158
FAX NUMBER: 201-614-0906

COMMENTS: They prefer "topics of general interest or those on which you have some special insight."

THE TRENTONIAN
Mark Stradling, Op-Ed Page Editor
600 Perry Street
Trenton, NJ 08618-3934

PAY SCALE:
WORD LENGTH:
COPYRIGHTED:
MUST LIVE IN AREA:
FREQUENCY:
PHONE NUMBER: 609-989-7800
FAX NUMBER: 609-393-6072

COMMENTS: They do not use freelance material, but do accept *Letters to the Editor*.

NEW MEXICO

ALBUQUERQUE JOURNAL
Bill Hume, Editorial Page Editor
7777 Jefferson, NE
Albuquerque, NM 87109-4360

PAY SCALE: $75
WORD LENGTH: 750
COPYRIGHTED: yes
MUST LIVE IN AREA: preferred
FREQUENCY: daily
PHONE NUMBER: 505-823-3800
FAX NUMBER: 505-823-3994

COMMENTS: Hume accepts freelance, but it's a "long shot." He wants articles specific to Albuquerque and New Mexico.

ALBUQUERQUE TRIBUNE
Jack Ehn, Editorial Page Editor
7777 Jefferson, NE
Albuquerque, NM 87109-4631

PAY SCALE: 0
WORD LENGTH: 700-800
COPYRIGHTED: yes
MUST LIVE IN AREA: yes
FREQUENCY: daily
PHONE NUMBER: 505-823-3600
FAX NUMBER: 505-823-3689

COMMENTS: Ehn wants pieces specific to the area.

NEW MEXICAN
Bill Waters, Editorial Page Editor
202 East Marcy
Sante Fe, NM 87501-2021

PAY SCALE:
WORD LENGTH:
COPYRIGHTED:
MUST LIVE IN AREA:
FREQUENCY:
PHONE NUMBER: 505-983-3303
FAX NUMBER: 505-986-9147

COMMENTS: They accept only commentary and do not pay or use many freelance Op-Ed submissions.

NEW YORK

THE BUFFALO NEWS
Barbara Ireland, Op-Ed Page Editor
One News Plaza
Buffalo, NY 14240

PAY SCALE: $40
WORD LENGTH: 800
COPYRIGHTED: yes
MUST LIVE IN AREA: yes
FREQUENCY: daily
PHONE NUMBER: 716-849-4444
FAX NUMBER: 716-856-5150

COMMENTS: They want articles written on local subjects only with strong connection to the area. Please submit by mail only.

NEW YORK DAILY NEWS
Robert Laird, Op-Ed Page Editor
220 East 42nd Street
New York, NY 10017-5858

PAY SCALE:
WORD LENGTH:
COPYRIGHTED:
MUST LIVE IN AREA:
FREQUENCY:
PHONE NUMBER: 212-210-2100
FAX NUMBER: 212-661-4675

COMMENTS: No reply after repeated attempts of phoning and faxing.

NEW YORK NEWSDAY
Ken Emerson, Op-Ed Page Editor
2 Park Avenue, 9th Floor
New York, NY 10016-5679

PAY SCALE: $150
WORD LENGTH: 750
COPYRIGHTED: first time rights
MUST LIVE IN AREA: no, but all pieces have a local angle
FREQUENCY: daily
PHONE NUMBER: 212-251-6941
FAX NUMBER: 212-447-0371

COMMENTS:

***Also see *Newsday* in the National Papers section at the front of the directory.

NEW YORK POST
Eric Breindel, Op-Ed Page Editor
210 South Street
New York, NY 10002-7889

PAY SCALE: $100
WORD LENGTH: 750-900
COPYRIGHTED: yes
MUST LIVE IN AREA: no
FREQUENCY: daily
PHONE NUMBER: 212-815-8610
FAX NUMBER: 212-732-4241

COMMENTS: Topics sought should be New York City related.

NEW YORK TIMES
Mike Levitas, Op-Ed Page Editor
229 West 43rd Street
New York, NY 10036-3959

PAY SCALE: $150
WORD LENGTH: 650
COPYRIGHTED: yes
MUST LIVE IN AREA: no
FREQUENCY: daily
PHONE NUMBER: 212-556-1234
FAX NUMBER: 212-556-4603

COMMENTS: Mike Levitas receives about 150 Op-Ed submissions daily. "What we're looking for is something that goes against the grain—something that's vigorously argued, timely, intelligent, lively, and persuasive," he says. A piece has a better shot if it's contradictory to the editorial page. No selection 'formula' exists. If you don't hear within a week or ten days, forget it.

ROCHESTER DEMOCRAT AND CHRONICLE
Dan Hall, Op-Ed Page Editor
55 Exchange Boulevard
Rochester, NY 14614-2075

PAY SCALE: 0
WORD LENGTH: 700-800
COPYRIGHTED: first time rights
MUST LIVE IN AREA: yes
FREQUENCY: daily
PHONE NUMBER: 716-232-7100
FAX NUMBER: 716-258-2487

COMMENTS: Hall recommends contacting Richard Prince to discuss specific ideas before spending much time on them. They prefer local topics of regional interest.

SYRACUSE POST-STANDARD

Tom Goll, Op-Ed Page Editor
P.O. Box 4818
Syracuse, NY 13221-4818

PAY SCALE: $25
WORD LENGTH: 1,200 or less
COPYRIGHTED: yes
MUST LIVE IN AREA: no, but greatly increases chances of publication
FREQUENCY: daily
PHONE NUMBER: 315-470-6045
FAX NUMBER: 315-470-3081

COMMENTS: Topics sought are those, "related to central New York," according to Goll.

NORTH CAROLINA

THE CHARLOTTE OBSERVER
Ed Williams, Editorial Page Editor
600 South Tryon Street
Charlotte, NC 28202-1800

PAY SCALE: $50
WORD LENGTH: 750
COPYRIGHTED: yes
MUST LIVE IN AREA: no, but it helps
FREQUENCY: daily
PHONE NUMBER: 704-358-5017
FAX NUMBER: 704-358-5022

COMMENTS: Jane Pope handles submissions. Williams is "only interested in localized (Carolinas) topics."

GREENSBORO NEWS & RECORD
Dave DuBuisson, Op-Ed Page Editor
P.O. Box 20848
Greensboro, NC 27420-0848

PAY SCALE: negotiable
WORD LENGTH: 800
COPYRIGHTED: yes
MUST LIVE IN AREA: no
FREQUENCY: daily
PHONE NUMBER: 910-373-7001
FAX NUMBER: 910-373-7382

COMMENTS: They pay for articles by negotiated agreement. You can live outside the area but write something of specific local interest.

THE NEWS & OBSERVER
Steve Ford, Op-Ed Page Editor
215 South McDowell Street
Raleigh, NC 27601-2929

PAY SCALE:
WORD LENGTH:
COPYRIGHTED:
MUST LIVE IN AREA:
FREQUENCY:
PHONE NUMBER: 919-829-4500
FAX NUMBER: 919-829-4824

COMMENTS: Ford gets so much material he did not feel the need to be listed in this directory.

WINSTON-SALEM JOURNAL
John D. Gates, Op-Ed Page Editor
416-20 North Marshall Street
Winston-Salem, NC 27101-2815

PAY SCALE: 0
WORD LENGTH: the "shorter the better;" maximum of 900
COPYRIGHTED: yes
MUST LIVE IN AREA: no, but preferred
FREQUENCY: daily
PHONE NUMBER: 910-727-7211
FAX NUMBER: 910-727-7315

COMMENTS: Gates will "look at anything." He terms himself "broad minded."

NORTH DAKOTA

THE FORUM
Jack Zaleski, Op-Ed Page Editor
101 North Fifth Street
Fargo, ND 58102-4826

PAY SCALE:
WORD LENGTH:
COPYRIGHTED:
MUST LIVE IN AREA:
FREQUENCY:
PHONE NUMBER: 701-235-7311
FAX NUMBER: 701-241-5487

COMMENTS: No reply after repeated attempts at faxing and phoning.

GRAND FORKS HERALD
Liz Fedor, Editorial Page Editor
114-120 North Fourth Street
Grand Forks, ND 58203-3722

PAY SCALE: 0
WORD LENGTH: 750
COPYRIGHTED: yes
MUST LIVE IN AREA: preferred
FREQUENCY: daily
PHONE NUMBER: 701-780-1100
FAX NUMBER: 701-780-1123

COMMENTS: Fedor uses regular local columnists so she does not pay or use much freelance material.

OHIO

AKRON BEACON JOURNAL
Bob Springer, Op-Ed Page Editor
44 East Exchange Street
Akron, OH 44328-0640

PAY SCALE: 0 unless solicited or pre-approved
WORD LENGTH: 700-800
COPYRIGHTED: yes
MUST LIVE IN AREA: no, but it must be exclusive to the market
FREQUENCY: daily
PHONE NUMBER: 216-996-3000
FAX NUMBER: 216-996-3053

COMMENTS: The *Journal* wants articles that are off the beaten path and offer a unique perspective to a national problem. A local tie-in helps.

CINCINNATI ENQUIRER
Peter Bronson, Editorial Page Editor
312 Elm Street
Cincinnati, OH 45202-2410

PAY SCALE: 0
WORD LENGTH: 500
COPYRIGHTED: yes
MUST LIVE IN AREA: yes
FREQUENCY: daily
PHONE NUMBER: 513-721-2700
FAX NUMBER: 513-768-8340

COMMENTS: Bronson receives so much freelance material he can "afford to be choosy"—and is. He has no budget and seldom uses material that is not from a local writer.

THE CINCINNATI POST
Robert White, Op-Ed Page Editor
125 East Court Street
Cincinnati, OH 45202-1214

PAY SCALE: $50
WORD LENGTH: 900
COPYRIGHTED: yes
MUST LIVE IN AREA: no, but it helps
FREQUENCY: Mon-Sat
PHONE NUMBER: 513-352-2000
FAX NUMBER: 513-621-3962

COMMENTS: Interested particularly in local and state issues.

CLEVELAND PLAIN DEALER
Brent Larkin, Op-Ed Page Editor
1801 Superior Avenue, NE
Cleveland, OH 44114-2192

PAY SCALE: $50
WORD LENGTH: 700-900
COPYRIGHTED: yes
MUST LIVE IN AREA: no
FREQUENCY: daily
PHONE NUMBER: 216-344-4500
FAX NUMBER: 216-694-6354

COMMENTS: Submissions for the Sunday Perspective Page can be 900-1,000 words.

DAYTON DAILY NEWS

Hap Cawood, Op-Ed Page Editor
45 South Ludlow Street
Dayton, OH 45402-1858

PAY SCALE: $35-50
WORD LENGTH: 400-800
COPYRIGHTED: yes
MUST LIVE IN AREA: preferably
FREQUENCY: daily
PHONE NUMBER: 513-225-2286
FAX NUMBER: 513-225-7302

COMMENTS: Cawood states, "almost all of the stuff we buy from freelancers is local. We rarely buy outside stuff because we have such an abundance. So we are not a very good freelance market."

TOLEDO BLADE

Tom Wellman, Editorial Page Editor
541 North Superior Street
Toledo, OH 43660-0002

PAY SCALE: 0 unless solicited, then up to $150
WORD LENGTH: not more than 800-900
COPYRIGHTED: yes
MUST LIVE IN AREA: no
FREQUENCY: daily
PHONE NUMBER: 419-245-6000
FAX NUMBER: 419-245-6439

COMMENTS: Wellman does not require that you live in the circulation area. He does "prefer a local tie-in. It is not essential though."

THE VINDICATOR

Dennis B. Mangan, Op-Ed Page Editor
107 Vindicator Square
Youngstown, OH 44501-0780

PAY SCALE: 0
WORD LENGTH: 400-500
COPYRIGHTED: yes
MUST LIVE IN AREA: yes
FREQUENCY: daily
PHONE NUMBER: 216-747-1471 ext 289
FAX NUMBER: 216-747-6712

COMMENTS:

OKLAHOMA

THE DAILY OKLAHOMAN
Jim Standard, Op-Ed Page Editor
P.O. Box 25125
Oklahoma, OK 73125-0125

PAY SCALE: 0, sometimes $20 if solicited
WORD LENGTH: 3 pages double-spaced
COPYRIGHTED: yes
MUST LIVE IN AREA: no
FREQUENCY: unscheduled, determined by space
PHONE NUMBER: 405-475-3311
FAX NUMBER: 405-475-3183

COMMENTS:

TULSA WORLD
Alex Adwan, Op-Ed Page Editor
315 South Main Mall
Tulsa, OK 74103-3674

PAY SCALE: 0
WORD LENGTH: open
COPYRIGHTED: yes
MUST LIVE IN AREA: preferred
FREQUENCY: Tues-Sat
PHONE NUMBER: 918-581-8300
FAX NUMBER: 918-581-8353

COMMENTS:

OREGON

THE REGISTER-GUARD
Don Robinson, Editorial Page Editor
975 High Street
Eugene, OR 97401-3273

PAY SCALE: seldom
WORD LENGTH: 800
COPYRIGHTED: yes
MUST LIVE IN AREA: no, but rarely run articles written from outside the area
FREQUENCY: daily
PHONE NUMBER: 503-485-1234
FAX NUMBER: 503-683-7631

COMMENTS: They usually don't pay for freelance Op-Ed submissions, but sometimes go up to $40. When they solicit a piece, they seek an individual with special credentials.

THE OREGONIAN
Glenn Davis, Forum Page Editor
1320 SW Broadway
Portland, OR 97201-3499

PAY SCALE: $75-350
WORD LENGTH: 900-1,000
COPYRIGHTED: yes
MUST LIVE IN AREA: no
FREQUENCY: daily
PHONE NUMBER: 503-221-8174
FAX NUMBER: 503-294-4193

COMMENTS: Articles, published on weekdays, should present new insights, analysis, or interpretations of current events or issues—supported by personal knowledge or expertise on the topic. Payment made after publication. Parody, poetry, and satire rarely accepted.

STATESMAN-JOURNAL
Don Scarborough, Op-Ed Page Editor
280 Church Street, NE
Salem, OR 97301-3762

PAY SCALE: 0 unless solicited
WORD LENGTH: 500
COPYRIGHTED: yes
MUST LIVE IN AREA: yes
FREQUENCY: daily
PHONE NUMBER: 503-399-6611
FAX NUMBER: 503-399-6706

COMMENTS:

PENNSYLVANIA

ALLENTOWN MORNING CALL
Van Cavett, Op-Ed Page Editor
P.O. Box 1260
Allentown, PA 18105-1260

PAY SCALE: $50
WORD LENGTH: 750-900
COPYRIGHTED: yes
MUST LIVE IN AREA: no
FREQUENCY: 6 days
PHONE NUMBER: 610-820-6728
FAX NUMBER: 610-820-6693

COMMENTS: Cavett wants "expertise in the field by the writer."

THE PATRIOT-NEWS
Wiley McKellar, Op-Ed Page Editor
812 King Boulevard
Harrisburg, PA 17101

PAY SCALE: 0, unless solicited
WORD LENGTH: 800 maximum, the shorter the better
COPYRIGHTED: yes
MUST LIVE IN AREA: no, but a local angle helps
FREQUENCY: daily, except Sat
PHONE NUMBER: 717-255-8100
FAX NUMBER: 717-255-8456

COMMENTS:

PHILADELPHIA DAILY NEWS

Don Harrison, Deputy Editor, Opinion Pages
400 North Broad Street
Philadelphia, PA 19130-4015

PAY SCALE: no
WORD LENGTH: 500
COPYRIGHTED: yes
MUST LIVE IN AREA: yes
FREQUENCY: five days a week
PHONE NUMBER: 215-854-5916
FAX NUMBER: 215-854-5691

COMMENTS: Harrison states, "Limited space and budget means we discourage outside submissions except for GuestOpinion, a locally-oriented, unpaid 500-word column."

PHILADELPHIA INQUIRER

Phil Joyce, Op-Ed Page Editor
400 North Broad Street
Philadelphia, PA 19130-4099

PAY SCALE: $100, sometimes more if solicited
WORD LENGTH: 750
COPYRIGHTED: first time use
MUST LIVE IN AREA: no
FREQUENCY: daily
PHONE NUMBER: 215-854-2000
FAX NUMBER: 215-854-4794

COMMENTS: "We consider our Commentary Page as a marketplace of ideas," says Joyce. "We have made an effort to attract more freelance pieces." They even wrote a column encouraging more contributions and reached out in the community to find pieces on a wide spectrum of subjects.

PITTSBURGH POST-GAZETTE
Mike Newman, Op-Ed Page Editor
50 Boulevard of the Allies
Pittsburgh, PA 15222

PAY SCALE: $60-100
WORD LENGTH: 800-900
COPYRIGHTED: yes, though you can offer one-time rights
MUST LIVE IN AREA: preferably
FREQUENCY: daily
PHONE NUMBER: 412-263-1661
FAX NUMBER: 412-263-2014

COMMENTS: Saturdays "Letters From" column uses casual, offbeat discussions on things from other areas and life experiences. "Black on Black" is for Black writers commenting on Black political or cultural topics.

PITTSBURGH PRESS
Mike McGough, Op-Ed Page Editor
34 Boulevard of the Allies
Pittsburgh, PA 15222-1200

PAY SCALE: $75
WORD LENGTH: 800 or less
COPYRIGHTED: yes, but you can reprint out of the area
MUST LIVE IN AREA: no
FREQUENCY: daily
PHONE NUMBER: 412-263-1441
FAX NUMBER: 412-263-2014

COMMENTS:

RHODE ISLAND

THE EVENING BULLETIN
Robert Whitcomb, Op-Ed Page Editor
75 Fountain Street
Providence, RI 02902-0050

PAY SCALE: $75-100
WORD LENGTH: 600-800
COPYRIGHTED: first time rights
MUST LIVE IN AREA: no
FREQUENCY: daily
PHONE NUMBER: 401-277-7000
FAX NUMBER: 401-277-7346

COMMENTS: Whitcomb "considers everything."

PROVIDENCE JOURNAL
Bob Whitcomb, Op-Ed Page Editor
75 Fountain Street
Providence, RI 02902

PAY SCALE: $40-100
WORD LENGTH: the shorter the better, between 700-800
COPYRIGHTED: yes
MUST LIVE IN AREA: no
FREQUENCY: daily, Letters page on Wednesday
PHONE NUMBER: 401-277-7000
FAX NUMBER: 401-277-7346

COMMENTS: To be accepted a piece has to be "mighty splendid and mighty important."

SOUTH CAROLINA

THE POST & COURIER
Barbara S. Williams, Op-Ed Page Editor
134 Columbus Street
Charleston, SC 29403-4800

PAY SCALE: up to $25
WORD LENGTH: 800
COPYRIGHTED: yes
MUST LIVE IN AREA: no
FREQUENCY: daily
PHONE NUMBER: 803-937-5526
FAX NUMBER: 803-937-5579

COMMENTS:

THE STATE
Brad Warthen, Op-Ed Page Editor
1401 Shop Road
Columbia, SC 29201-4843

PAY SCALE: nothing, unless it's really special
WORD LENGTH: 600
COPYRIGHTED: yes
MUST LIVE IN AREA: no, but we prefer it
FREQUENCY: daily
PHONE NUMBER: 803-771-8468
FAX NUMBER: 803-771-8639

COMMENTS:

GREENVILLE NEWS
Thomas Inman, Op-Ed Page Editor
305 South Main Street
Greenville, SC 29601-2640

PAY SCALE:
WORD LENGTH:
COPYRIGHTED:
MUST LIVE IN AREA:
FREQUENCY:
PHONE NUMBER: 803-298-4100
FAX NUMBER: 803-298-4395

COMMENTS: Inman uses credential experts in South Carolina regrading area issues and syndicated material. Rarely uses freelance submissions.

SOUTH DAKOTA

RAPID CITY JOURNAL
Ted Brockish, Editorial Page Editor
507 Main Street
Rapid City, SD 57701-2777

PAY SCALE: 0
WORD LENGTH: 800
COPYRIGHTED: yes
MUST LIVE IN AREA: no
FREQUENCY: Forum page in Saturday's edition
PHONE NUMBER: 605-394-8091
FAX NUMBER: 605-394-4610

COMMENTS:

TENNESSEE

CHATTANOOGA NEWS-FREE PRESS
Lee Anderson, Op-Ed Page Editor
400 East 11th Street
Chattanooga, TN 37401-1447

PAY SCALE: 0
WORD LENGTH: 500-600
COPYRIGHTED: no
MUST LIVE IN AREA: no
FREQUENCY: almost daily
PHONE NUMBER: 615-757-6300
FAX NUMBER: 615-757-6383

COMMENTS: Anderson doesn't use most unsolicited columns.

KNOXVILLE NEWS-SENTINEL
Hoyt Canady, Op-Ed Page Editor
208 West Church
Knoxville, TN 37902-1683

PAY SCALE: 0
WORD LENGTH:
COPYRIGHTED:
MUST LIVE IN AREA:
FREQUENCY:
PHONE NUMBER: 615-523-3131
FAX NUMBER: 615-521-8186

COMMENTS: Canady has limited space and isn't encouraging because he uses freelance submissions infrequently.

MEMPHIS COMMERCIAL APPEAL
Richard McFalls, Op-Ed Page Editor
495 Union Avenue
Memphis, TN 38103-3221

PAY SCALE: not much
WORD LENGTH: 700-750 tops
COPYRIGHTED: yes
MUST LIVE IN AREA: preferred
FREQUENCY: daily
PHONE NUMBER: 901-529-2211
FAX NUMBER: 901-529-2362

COMMENTS: They prefer experts in the field from their area to submit material. Don't use a lot of freelance material.

THE NASHVILLE BANNER
Sue McClure, Op-Ed Page Editor
1100 Broadway
Nashville, TN 37203-3116

PAY SCALE: 0
WORD LENGTH: 700
COPYRIGHTED: yes
MUST LIVE IN AREA: yes
FREQUENCY: daily
PHONE NUMBER: 615-259-8800
FAX NUMBER: 615-259-8890

COMMENTS: McClure is looking for general interest material.

THE TENNESSEAN
Terry Quillen, Op-Ed Page Editor
1100 Broadway
Nashville, TN 37203-3116

PAY SCALE: 0
WORD LENGTH: 650-800
COPYRIGHTED: yes
MUST LIVE IN AREA: yes
FREQUENCY: Mon-Fri, Sun
PHONE NUMBER: 615-259-8000
FAX NUMBER: 615-259-8093

COMMENTS: Quillen rarely uses unsolicited essays. He gets more from syndicated columnists than he needs. He prefers to use local writers who write about local issues out of personal experience.

TEXAS

AUSTIN AMERICAN STATESMAN
Arnold Garcia, Op-Ed Page Editor
P.O. Box 607
Austin, TX 78767

PAY SCALE: 0
WORD LENGTH: 600 is outer limit
COPYRIGHTED: yes
MUST LIVE IN AREA: strongly preferred
FREQUENCY: daily
PHONE NUMBER: 512-445-3500
FAX NUMBER: 512-445-3679

COMMENTS: Garcia is very proud of his column and feels it is "balanced." Austin is the state capital and a university town so he gets flooded with good local pieces, thus rarely uses out of area writers. He will, however, if the piece makes his "socks roll up and down." Has limited space but does consider all submissions. Is willing to talk to writers about ideas for submissions.

CORPUS CHRISTI CALLER-TIMES
Jerry Norman, Op-Ed Page Editor
820 North Lower Broadway
Corpus Christi, TX 78401-2025

PAY SCALE: 0
WORD LENGTH: 600-1200
COPYRIGHTED: yes
MUST LIVE IN AREA: no
FREQUENCY: 2 pages run daily
PHONE NUMBER: 512-884-2011
FAX NUMBER: 512-886-3732

COMMENTS: Norman is flexible with word length. It depends on the subject matter, the writer, and how important the paper feels the subject is to their readership. He receives a lot of material over the transom, from several local universities, and from local politicians.

THE DALLAS MORNING NEWS
Carolyn Barta, Op-Ed Page Editor
508 Young
Dallas, TX 75202

PAY SCALE: $75, more for Sunday
WORD LENGTH: 750
COPYRIGHTED: yes
MUST LIVE IN AREA: no, but given preference
FREQUENCY: daily
PHONE NUMBER: 214-977-8222
FAX NUMBER: 214-977-8776

COMMENTS: Barta wants pieces to fill the "gaps in coverage." They typically look for public policy pieces. No humor. Include a tag line and your social security number. If your piece is used, you will be asked to supply a photo.

EL PASO TIMES
Elaine Ayala, Editorial Page Editor
P.O. Box 20
El Paso, TX 79901-1426

PAY SCALE: 0
WORD LENGTH: 600-800
COPYRIGHTED: yes
MUST LIVE IN AREA: no, but given preference
FREQUENCY: daily
PHONE NUMBER: 915-546-6100
FAX NUMBER: 915-546-6415

COMMENTS: Ayala does use guest column pieces for extended *Letters to the Editor*. Occasionally, they'll ask for a piece from someone with expertise in a specific area.

FORT WORTH STAR-TELEGRAM
Ann Thompson, Op-Ed Page Editor
400 West Seventh Street
Fort Worth, TX 76102-4793

PAY SCALE: $75
WORD LENGTH: 900
COPYRIGHTED: yes
MUST LIVE IN AREA: yes
FREQUENCY: daily
PHONE NUMBER: 817-390-7400
FAX NUMBER: 817-390-7789

COMMENTS: Thompson recently lost ¼ of her space, so she has very little room on the Op-Ed pages. If you strictly want to write a point of view article on a timely topic you're better off the submitting to the *Letters to the Editor*. On Sundays they have more space and it is highly competitive. Your piece needs to be well argued, have an original perspective, and a regional/local point. Thompson doesn't mind humor if its about the news and "it's the sugar that makes the medicine go down."

HOUSTON CHRONICLE
Frank Michael, Op-Ed Page Editor
801 Texas Street
Houston, TX 77002

PAY SCALE: 0, unless solicited
WORD LENGTH: 700-900
COPYRIGHTED: first time rights, don't submit to Houston area simultaneously
MUST LIVE IN AREA: no
FREQUENCY: daily, separate six-page section on Sunday
PHONE NUMBER: 713-220-7171
FAX NUMBER: 713-220-6575

COMMENTS: Michael won't pay unless solicited. Forum pieces that are written out of self-interest don't receive payment. He publishes 1,100 pieces a year, and reads 10-15 more to select those. He wants strong opinion pieces as opposed to feature or research articles. You can fax or mail submissions. If you don't hear in two-three days, call and inquire.

THE HOUSTON POST
Fred King, Op-Ed Page Editor
4747 Southwest Freeway
Houston, TX 77027

PAY SCALE: $40-100
WORD LENGTH: 850
COPYRIGHTED: yes, but buys only one-time rights in their circulation area
MUST LIVE IN AREA: no, but preferred
FREQUENCY: daily
PHONE NUMBER: 713-840-5823
FAX NUMBER: 713-840-6722

COMMENTS: No particular category of topics, but wants exclusive rights in Houston, Dallas, San Antonio, and Austin.

SAN ANTONIO EXPRESS-NEWS
Sterlin Holmsley, Op-Ed Page Editor
P.O. Box 2171
San Antonio, TX 78297-2171

PAY SCALE: 0
WORD LENGTH: 700
COPYRIGHTED: yes
MUST LIVE IN AREA: yes
FREQUENCY: daily
PHONE NUMBER: 210-255-7411
FAX NUMBER: 210-229-9268

COMMENTS: Holmsley doesn't use freelance material often; he has a string of local contributors.

UTAH

DESERET NEWS
Jay Evensen, Op-Ed Page Editor
30 East First South
Salt Lake City, UT 84111-1902

PAY SCALE: 0
WORD LENGTH: 2-3 typed pages
COPYRIGHTED: yes
MUST LIVE IN AREA: no
FREQUENCY: daily
PHONE NUMBER: 801-237-2100
FAX NUMBER: 801-237-2121

COMMENTS: Evensen uses pieces from credentialed experts.

THE SALT LAKE TRIBUNE
Harry Fuller, Op-Ed Page Editor
143 South Main Street
Salt Lake City, UT 84111-1917

PAY SCALE: 0
WORD LENGTH: 800-900
COPYRIGHTED: yes
MUST LIVE IN AREA: no
FREQUENCY: daily
PHONE NUMBER: 801-237-2021
FAX NUMBER: 801-521-9418

COMMENTS: The Op-Ed page is issue-oriented so they prefer submissions written by experts in their field.

VERMONT

BURLINGTON FREE PRESS
Jill Kirsch, Op-Ed Page Editor
191 College Street
Burlington, VT 05401-8300

PAY SCALE: 0
WORD LENGTH: 600-800, not written in stone
COPYRIGHTED: yes
MUST LIVE IN AREA: locals are given strong preference
FREQUENCY: daily
PHONE NUMBER: 802-863-3441
FAX NUMBER: 802-862-1802

COMMENTS:

RUTLAND HERALD
David Moats, Editorial Page Editor
P.O. Box 347
Rutland, VT 05701-4000

PAY SCALE: 0
WORD LENGTH: under 750
COPYRIGHTED: yes
MUST LIVE IN AREA: yes
FREQUENCY: 2 pages per week
PHONE NUMBER: 802-775-5511
FAX NUMBER: 802-775-2423

COMMENTS: Moats requires that submissions relate to Vermont.

VIRGINIA

THE FREE-LANCE STAR
Larry Evans, Editorial Page Editor
616 Amelia Street
Fredricksburg, VA 22401

PAY SCALE: 0
WORD LENGTH: 750
COPYRIGHTED: yes
MUST LIVE IN AREA: no
FREQUENCY: Mon-Sat
PHONE NUMBER: 703-373-5000
FAX NUMBER: 703-373-8450

COMMENTS: Evans *doesn't* want "predictable opinions on predictable topics."

THE LEDGER-STAR
John Barnes, Op-Ed Page Editor
150 West Brambleton Avenue
Norfolk, VA 23510-2075

PAY SCALE: 0
WORD LENGTH: 750 maximum
COPYRIGHTED: yes
MUST LIVE IN AREA: no
FREQUENCY: daily
PHONE NUMBER: 804-446-2000
FAX NUMBER: 804-446-2414

COMMENTS: Inclined to use articles with a local flavor. (The *Ledger-Star* is an afternoon edition, the *Virginian Pilot* the morning edition).

VIRGINIAN PILOT
John Barnes, Op-Ed Page Editor
150 West Brambleton Avenue
Norfolk, VA 23510-2075

PAY SCALE: 0
WORD LENGTH: 750 maximum
COPYRIGHTED: yes
MUST LIVE IN AREA: no
FREQUENCY: daily
PHONE NUMBER: 804-446-2000
FAX NUMBER: 804-446-2414

COMMENTS: Inclined to use articles with a local flavor. (The *Virginian Pilot* is the morning edition, *the Ledger-Star* the afternoon edition).

RICHMOND TIMES-DISPATCH
Bob Holland, Op-Ed Page Editor
333 Grace Street
Richmond, VA 23219-6100

PAY SCALE: 0
WORD LENGTH: 750
COPYRIGHTED: first-time rights
MUST LIVE IN AREA: no
FREQUENCY: daily
PHONE NUMBER: 804-469-6000
FAX NUMBER: 804-775-8059

COMMENTS: Holland is willing to consider freelance, but he doesn't have a lot of room so make it good.

ROANOKE TIMES & WORLD-NEWS

Betty Strother, Op-Ed Page Editor
201 Campbell Avenue, SW
Roanoke, VA 24011-1105

PAY SCALE: 0
WORD LENGTH: 750-850
COPYRIGHTED: yes
MUST LIVE IN AREA: no
FREQUENCY: Mon-Fri, Sun
PHONE NUMBER: 703-981-3100
FAX NUMBER: 703-981-3346

COMMENTS: Strother wants opinions that are well read and create debate. She likes submissions to be topical and on a variety of things. Prefers people from outside the area be credentialed and bring in a new perspective.

WASHINGTON

THE BREMERTON SUN
Mike Phillips, Editorial Page Editor
545 Fifth Street
Bremerton, WA 98310-1413

PAY SCALE: 0
WORD LENGTH: 600-800
COPYRIGHTED: no
MUST LIVE IN AREA: yes
FREQUENCY: daily
PHONE NUMBER: 206-792-9201
FAX NUMBER: 206-479-7681

COMMENTS:

THE HERALD
Joe Copeland, Editorial Page Editor
P.O. Box 930
Everett, WA 98206-0930

PAY SCALE:
WORD LENGTH:
COPYRIGHTED:
MUST LIVE IN AREA:
FREQUENCY:
PHONE NUMBER:
FAX NUMBER:

COMMENTS: Copeland commented, "Sorry, but we aren't currently taking freelance."

SEATTLE POST-INTELLIGENCER

Charles J. Dunsire, Op-Ed Page Editor
101 Elliott Avenue, W
Seattle, WA 98119-4220

PAY SCALE: $75-100
WORD LENGTH: 750-800
COPYRIGHTED: yes
MUST LIVE IN AREA: no
FREQUENCY: 4 times per week
PHONE NUMBER: 206-448-8387:
FAX NUMBER: 206-448-8184

COMMENTS: Limited space and budget, but will consider general interest subjects.

SEATTLE TIMES

James Vesely, Op-Ed Page Editor
P.O. Box 70
Seattle, WA 98111

PAY SCALE: $50-100
WORD LENGTH: 800
COPYRIGHTED: yes
MUST LIVE IN AREA: no
FREQUENCY: Mon-Fri
PHONE NUMBER: 206-464-2323
FAX NUMBER: 206-382-6760

COMMENTS: Vesely is interested primarily in regional issues, but will consider national issues. No humor or satire please.

SPOKESMAN REVIEW
Doug Floyd, Op-Ed Page Editor
West 999 Riverside
Spokane, WA 99201

PAY SCALE: 0
WORD LENGTH: 400
COPYRIGHTED: yes
MUST LIVE IN AREA: yes
FREQUENCY: daily
PHONE NUMBER: 509-459-5430
FAX NUMBER: 509-459-5482

COMMENTS: Want to be labeled a "prize winning" writer? The editorial board of this paper nominates one reader essay each week for their Golden Pen Award. This essay appears on Monday. Each month the board chooses an overall winner who receives a 10-karat gold Cross pen. The weekly From Both Sides column examines issues from two points of view. The purpose is to ease the frustration of readers who disagree with the paper's editorial positions and to literally "turn over the opinion pages to the community," says managing editor Chris Peck.

MORNING NEWS TRIBUNE
John Komen, Editor
1950 South State Street
Tacoma, WA 98405-2860

PAY SCALE: 0
WORD LENGTH: 800-1,000
COPYRIGHTED: yes
MUST LIVE IN AREA: no
FREQUENCY: daily
PHONE NUMBER: 206-597-8631
FAX NUMBER: 206-597-8274

COMMENTS:

WEST VIRGINIA

CHARLESTON DAILY MAIL
Johanna L. Maurice, Op-Ed Page Editor
1001 Virginia Street East
Charleston, WV 25301-2895

PAY SCALE: minimal (whatever that means)
WORD LENGTH: 1,000
COPYRIGHTED: yes
MUST LIVE IN AREA: no
FREQUENCY: daily
PHONE NUMBER: 304-348-5140
FAX NUMBER: 304-348-4847

COMMENTS: The *Daily Mail* has limited Op-Ed space so make it topical or it won't be considered.

CHARLESTON GAZETTE
Dan Radnacker, Op-Ed Page Editor
1001 Virginia Street East
Charleston, WV 25301-2895

PAY SCALE: varies
WORD LENGTH: 2-3 pages
COPYRIGHTED: yes
MUST LIVE IN AREA: no
FREQUENCY: daily
PHONE NUMBER: 304-348-5100
FAX NUMBER: 304-348-1233

COMMENTS:

WISCONSIN

GREEN BAY PRESS-GAZETTE
Bob Woresner, Opinion Page Editor
P.O. Box 19430
Green Bay, WI 54307-9430

PAY SCALE: 0
WORD LENGTH: 600 maximum
COPYRIGHTED: yes
MUST LIVE IN AREA: yes
FREQUENCY: Sun
PHONE NUMBER: 414-435-4411
FAX NUMBER: 434-431-8379

COMMENTS: Op-Ed pieces are run as guest columns.

THE CAPITAL TIMES
Phil Haslanger, Op-Ed Page Editor
P.O. Box 8060
Madison, WI 53708

PAY SCALE: $25
WORD LENGTH: 600-700
COPYRIGHTED: no
MUST LIVE IN AREA: yes
FREQUENCY: daily
PHONE NUMBER: 608-252-6400
FAX NUMBER: 608-252-6445

COMMENTS: Haslanger wants pieces that "address local issues, have a personal dimension, and are well told."

MILWAUKEE JOURNAL
Jim Cattey, Op-Ed Page Editor
333 West State Street
Milwaukee, WI 53203-1309

PAY SCALE:
WORD LENGTH:
COPYRIGHTED:
MUST LIVE IN AREA:
FREQUENCY:
PHONE NUMBER: 414-224-2000
FAX NUMBER: 414-224-2047

COMMENTS: Sue Ryan the Assistant Editorial Page Editor responded, "I'm sorry, but we just don't have room for freelance Op-Ed material."

MILWAUKEE SENTINEL
Marilyn Kucer, Op-Ed Page Editor
918 North Fourth Street
Milwaukee, WI 53201-1500

PAY SCALE:
WORD LENGTH:
COPYRIGHTED:
MUST LIVE IN AREA:
FREQUENCY:
PHONE NUMBER: 414-224-2194
FAX NUMBER: 414-224-2049

COMMENTS: They do not accept freelance Op-Ed submissions.

WYOMING

CASPER STAR-TRIBUNE

Charles Levindowsky, Op-Ed Page Editor
170 Star Lane
Casper, WY 82604-2883

PAY SCALE: 0
WORD LENGTH: 750-1,000
COPYRIGHTED: yes
MUST LIVE IN AREA: no
FREQUENCY: daily
PHONE NUMBER: 307-266-0500
FAX NUMBER: 307-266-0501

COMMENTS: Levindowsky is most interested in issues that deal with the region. He will accept pieces from people with expertise in an area. "Play to your strengths:" if you take a serious perspective he doesn't care what side of the issue you argue as long as your facts are straight. Not interested in humor. He wants serious issues that give "perspective to the news people are reading about."

Part III

CANADIAN NEWSPAPERS BY PROVINCE

ALBERTA

CALGARY HERALD
Neil Haesler, Op-Ed Page Editor
215 16th Street, SE
Calgary, Alberta
CANADA T2P 0W8

PAY SCALE: $75-150
WORD LENGTH: 1500
COPYRIGHTED: yes
MUST LIVE IN AREA: no
FREQUENCY: daily
PHONE NUMBER: 403-235-7100
FAX NUMBER: 403-235-7379

COMMENTS: Haesler doesn't prefer any specific topic, he likes "everything."

THE EDMONTON JOURNAL
Duart Farquharson, Op-Ed Page Editor
10006 101st Street
Edmonton, Alberta
CANADA T5J 2S6

PAY SCALE: $75-100
WORD LENGTH: 700-800
COPYRIGHTED: yes
MUST LIVE IN AREA: no, but local writers are given preference
FREQUENCY: daily
PHONE NUMBER: 403-429-5100
FAX NUMBER: 403-429-5500

COMMENTS: They use a lot of wire services so make it topical and very interesting.

BRITISH COLUMBIA

THE PROVINCE
James McNulty, Editorial Page Editor
2250 Granville Street
Vancouver, British Columbia
CANADA V6H 3G2

PAY SCALE: $150-250
WORD LENGTH: 900-1,000
COPYRIGHTED: yes
MUST LIVE IN AREA: yes
FREQUENCY: Sun
PHONE NUMBER: 604-732-2063
FAX NUMBER: 604-732-2720

COMMENTS: *The Province* has two different sections that use freelance material, the Opinion Column and the Sunday Inside Pages. An Opinion Column would be shorter at 600 words and pay somewhere around $250. The Sunday Inside Pages are written by regular columnists so there is not much use for freelance submissions.

THE VANCOUVER SUN
Alex MacGillivray, Op-Ed Page Editor
2250 Granville Street
Vancouver, British Columbia
CANADA V6H 3G2

PAY SCALE: $50-125
WORD LENGTH: 800, double-spaced
COPYRIGHTED: yes
MUST LIVE IN AREA: no
FREQUENCY: daily
PHONE NUMBER: 604-732-2111
FAX NUMBER: 604-732-2323

COMMENTS: Do not submit articles regarding national affairs, they have their own writers for that.

MANITOBA

WINNIPEG FREE PRESS
John DaFoe, Op-Ed Page Editor
1355 Mountain Avenue
Winnipeg, Manitoba
CANADA R2X 3B6

PAY SCALE:
WORD LENGTH:
COPYRIGHTED:
MUST LIVE IN AREA:
FREQUENCY:
PHONE NUMBER: 204-697-7000
FAX NUMBER: 204-697-7412

COMMENTS: No response after repeated efforts to contact.

NEW BRUNSWICK

THE EVENING TIMES-GLOBE
Gerald Childs, Executive Editor
210 Crown Street
St. John, New Brunswick
CANADA E2L 3V8

PAY SCALE: varies
WORD LENGTH: doesn't matter, not too long
COPYRIGHTED: yes
MUST LIVE IN AREA: no
FREQUENCY: daily
PHONE NUMBER: 506-632-8888
FAX NUMBER: 506-648-2652

COMMENTS:

NEWFOUNDLAND

THE EVENING TELEGRAM
Moira Baird, Op-Ed Page Editor
P.O. Box 5970
St. John's, Newfoundland
CANADA A1C 5X7

PAY SCALE: 0
WORD LENGTH: 600
COPYRIGHTED: first time rights
MUST LIVE IN AREA: no
FREQUENCY: daily
PHONE NUMBER: 709-364-2323
FAX NUMBER: 709-364-9333

COMMENTS: Baird prefers articles with a local angle. They don't usually pay for submissions because they get so many "freebies."

NOVA SCOTIA

THE CHRONICLE-HERALD
Bev Dauphnee, Op-Ed Page Editor
10 Lawrence Street, Box 280
Amherst, Nova Scotia
CANADA B4H 3Z2

PAY SCALE: $0-75
WORD LENGTH: 700-900
COPYRIGHTED: yes
MUST LIVE IN AREA: no
FREQUENCY: daily
PHONE NUMBER: 902-426-2811
FAX NUMBER: 902-426-3014

COMMENTS: Dauphnee rarely pays unless an article is exceptional. She prefers local topics.

ONTARIO

THE HAMILTON SPECTATOR
Gary Hall, Op-Ed Page Editor
44 Fid Street
Hamilton, Ontario
CANADA L8N 3G3

PAY SCALE: $50-200
WORD LENGTH: within reason
COPYRIGHTED: first time rights
MUST LIVE IN AREA: yes
FREQUENCY: daily
PHONE NUMBER: 416-526-3333
FAX NUMBER: 416-521-8986

COMMENTS:

THE LONDON FREE PRESS
Helen Connell, Op-Ed Page Editor
369 York Street
London, Ontario
CANADA N6A 4G1

PAY SCALE: $25-400
WORD LENGTH: 600-800, The Saturday Forum: 1,000-1,200
COPYRIGHTED: varies
MUST LIVE IN AREA: preferred
FREQUENCY: daily
PHONE NUMBER: 519-679-1111
FAX NUMBER: 519-667-4528

COMMENTS:

THE CITIZEN
Peter Calamai, Editorial Page Editor
1101 Baxter Road
Ottawa, Ontario
CANADA K2C 3M4

PAY SCALE: $100-150
WORD LENGTH: 800-850
COPYRIGHTED: first time rights
MUST LIVE IN AREA: preferred
FREQUENCY: daily
PHONE NUMBER: 613-829-9100
FAX NUMBER: 613-726-1198

COMMENTS: They prefer articles that are topical and timely. Wants to hear a variety of voices.

THE GLOBE & MAIL
Warren Clements, Op-Ed Page Editor
444 Front Street West
Toronto, Ontario
CANADA M5V 2S9

PAY SCALE: varies
WORD LENGTH: 800
COPYRIGHTED: yes
MUST LIVE IN AREA: no
FREQUENCY: daily
PHONE NUMBER: 416-585-5225
FAX NUMBER: 416-585-5085

COMMENTS: Submissions for the Commentary Page are coming in droves, so make it unique.

THE TORONTO SUN
John Downing, Op-Ed Page Editor
333 King Street East
Toronto, Ontario
CANADA M5A 3X5

PAY SCALE:
WORD LENGTH:
COPYRIGHTED: yes
MUST LIVE IN AREA: no
FREQUENCY: daily
PHONE NUMBER: 416-947-2222
FAX NUMBER: 416-947-3228

COMMENTS: They rarely use freelance, but give it a try.

QUEBEC

LE JOURNAL DE MONTREAL
Jean V. DuFresne, Editorial Page Editor
4545 Frontenac
Montreal, Quebec
CANADA H2H 2R7

PAY SCALE:
WORD LENGTH:
COPYRIGHTED:
MUST LIVE IN AREA:
FREQUENCY:
PHONE NUMBER: 514-521-4545
FAX NUMBER: 514-521-4416

COMMENTS: No response to repeated phone and fax inquiries.

THE GAZETTE
Jennifer Robinson, Op-Ed Page Editor
250 St. Antoine Street, West
Montreal, Quebec
CANADA H2Y 3R7

PAY SCALE: varies
WORD LENGTH: 800-1,000
COPYRIGHTED: yes
MUST LIVE IN AREA: no
FREQUENCY: daily
PHONE NUMBER: 514-987-2462
FAX NUMBER: 514-987-2433

COMMENTS:

LA PRESSE
Alain Dubuc, Editorial Page Editor
7 Ouest Rue St. Jacques
Montreal, Quebec
CANADA H2Y 1K9

PAY SCALE:
WORD LENGTH:
COPYRIGHTED:
MUST LIVE IN AREA:
FREQUENCY:
PHONE NUMBER: 514-285-7272
FAX NUMBER: 514-285-6808

COMMENTS: They do not use freelance Op-Ed.

LE SOLEIL
Raymond Giroux, Op-Ed Page Editor
390 St. Vallier East
Quebec, Quebec
CANADA G1K 7J6

PAY SCALE:
WORD LENGTH:
COPYRIGHTED:
MUST LIVE IN AREA:
FREQUENCY:
PHONE NUMBER: 418-647-3233
FAX NUMBER: 418-647-3374

COMMENTS: Ignored repeated calls and faxes requesting information.

SASKATCHEWAN

REGINA LEADER POST
David Green, Op-Ed Page Editor
1964 Park Street
Regina, Saskatchewan
CANADA S4P 3G4

PAY SCALE: $40-60
WORD LENGTH: 600-700
COPYRIGHTED: yes
MUST LIVE IN AREA: no
FREQUENCY: daily
PHONE NUMBER: 306-565-8211
FAX NUMBER: 306-565-2588

COMMENTS: Green doesn't want "frivolous material." Humor is fine if it doesn't assassinate anyone.

THE STAR PHOENIX
Lawrence Thoner, Op-Ed Page Editor
204 Fifth Avenue North
Saskatoon, Saskatchewan
CANADA S7K 2P1

PAY SCALE: $75
WORD LENGTH: 650-700
COPYRIGHTED: first time rights only
MUST LIVE IN AREA: yes
FREQUENCY: Thurs, Fri
PHONE NUMBER: 306-664-8231
FAX NUMBER: 306-664-0437

COMMENTS: Thoner uses local writers and tries to accommodate everyone eventually.

INDEX

ABOUT THE AUTHOR/COMPILER

Marilyn Ross is the author or co-author of 11 books, including the popular *Big Ideas for Small Service Businesses*. She and her husband, Tom, founded Accelerated Business Images—a public relations and advertising firm that specializes in helping small businesses with "Spot Marketing Alternatives." These quick fix programs offer long lasting results for start-ups or firms desiring to reposition themselves or enhance their publicity potential.

The Rosses are members of the National Speakers Association and are frequently called upon to give their unique team presentation to organizations, associations, and corporations. They give seminars and workshops on such topics as "Unabashed Power ProMOTION" and "Top Drawer Marketing Strategies for Bottom Line Results."

Marilyn Ross also belongs to the American Society of Journalists and Authors and the Authors Guild. She is included in *Contemporary Authors, The World Who's Who of Women, U.S. Writers, Editors & Poets, Who's Who in the West,* and *Who's Who of American Women.* She can be reached at the address below:

Accelerated Business Images
P.O. Box 1500-OPED
Buena Vista, CO 81211-1500
(719) 395-2459

GIVE A COPY OF THIS DIRECTORY TO FRIENDS & COLLEAGUES!

☐ **YES,** send _ copies of the *National Directory of Newspaper Op-Ed Pages* at $19.95 each plus $3 for shipping and handling. (Colorado residents please add $1.40 sales tax).

Responsible for promoting a business or professional practice? You need Marilyn and Tom Rosses' *Big Ideas for Small Service Businesses.* It shows how to publicize, advertise, and maximize a service business or professional practice. No fluff here; 283 ideas to get you to the core realities behind success. Scores of examples of what works and powerful models serve as your written brainstorming partner. Loaded with useful checklists and samples, it's also a real bargain.
☐ **YES,** *Big Ideas for Small Service Businesses* sounds like a great investment. Send me _____ copies at $15.95 plus $3 for shipping and handling. (Colorado residents please add $1.17 sales tax.)

Have you authored a book or do you work with someone who has? Every author and book publicist needs *The Complete Guide to Self-Publishing.* Written by award-winning authors Tom and Marilyn Ross, it tells everything you need to know to successfully write, produce, promote, and *sell* books. The newly revised and expanded 1994 edition has over 400 pages chock-full of proven ideas and practical pointers. Also includes sample sales letters and forms, checklists, plus a comprehensive appendix, bibliography, glossary, index, and Publishing Timetable to keep you on course.
☐ **YES,** I want ___copies of *The Complete Guide to Self-Publishing* at just $18.99 each, plus $3 shipping and handling. (Colorado residents please add $1.33 sales tax.)

Seeking solutions to problems in marketing, writing, or publishing? The Maverick Mail Order Bookstore comes to the rescue! Free catalog lists dozens of books in these categories and more. They're the cream of the crop in their subject areas. By offering this unique collection of books by mail, we make it easy for busy people to find what they need to be more successful.

☐ ____ **YES,** I want a copy of the *Maverick Mail Order Bookstore* catalog. (Please send a #10 self-addressed envelope with two first class stamps.)

ORDER FORM

Name _____

Organization _____

Address _____ Phone _____

City/State/Zip _____

Signature _____

Charge my ☐ VISA ☐ MasterCard Number _____ Exp date _____

To order: COMMUNICATION CREATIVITY, Box 909-OPED, Buena Vista, CO 81211
Fax orders: 303-395-8374.

Call credit card orders to 1-800-331-8355 ■ Ask about our quantity discounts